KEY MANAGEMENT
DECISIONS

MANAGEMENT
MASTERCLASS

KEY MANAGEMENT
DECISIONS

Tools and techniques of the
executive decision-maker

DES DEARLOVE

FINANCIAL TIMES
PITMAN PUBLISHING

FINANCIAL TIMES
MANAGEMENT
LONDON · SAN FRANCISCO
KUALA LUMPUR · JOHANNESBURG

*Financial Times Management delivers the knowledge,
skills and understanding that enable students,
managers and organisation to achieve their ambitions,
whatever their needs, whatever they are.*

London Office:
128 Long Acre, London WC2E 9AN
Tel: +44 (0)171 447 2000
Fax: +44 (0)171 240 5771
Website: www.ftmanagement.com

A Division of Financial Times Professional Limited

First published in Great Britain in 1998

© Pearson Professional Limited 1998

The right of Des Dearlove to be identified as author
of this work has been asserted by him in accordance
with the Copyright, Designs and Patents Act 1988.

ISBN 0 273 63009 1

British Library Cataloguing in Publication Data
A CIP catalogue record for this book can be obtained from the British Library

All rights reserved; no part of this publication may be reproduced, stored
in a retrieval system, or transmitted in any form or by any means, electronic,
mechanical, photocopying, recording, or otherwise without either the prior
written permission of the Publishers or a licence permitting restricted copying
in the United Kingdom issued by the Copyright Licensing Agency Ltd,
90 Tottenham Court Road, London W1P 0LP. This book may not be lent,
resold, hired out or otherwise disposed of by way of trade in any form
of binding or cover other than that in which it is published, without the
prior consent of the Publishers.

10 9 8 7 6 5 4 3 2

Typeset by Pantek Arts, Maidstone, Kent.
Printed and bound in Great Britain by Redwood Books, Trowbridge, Wiltshire.

The Publishers' policy is to use paper manufactured from sustainable forests.

The Author

Des Dearlove is a management and business journalist. Former editor of *The Times* Recruitment section, he now writes the weekly 'Management Plus' column and edits *The Times* MBA reports. His articles have also appeared in a number of other newspapers including *The Sunday Times* and the *Financial Times*.

Des contributes to a wide variety of business magazines and journals including *TIME Magazine* and *Human Resources Magazine*. He has co-authored several books on management best practice.

Contents

Acknowledgements

All books are written by people standing on the shoulders of others, and I am particularly grateful for the view afforded me by all those quoted in the text.

I am also indebted to the following individuals and organisations for permission to reproduce copyrighted material:

Terry Brake
Peter Reilly and Penny Tamkin, at the Institute of Employment Studies
Mary Lacity and Leslie Willcocks, at Templeton College, Oxford.

Key for icons

The following icons and the concepts they represent have been used throughout this book.

 Action or take note

 Key idea

 Case study

 Checklist

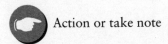 References

Introduction

'Executives do many things in addition to making decisions. But only executives make decisions. The first managerial skill is, therefore, the making of effective decisions'
PETER DRUCKER, management writer
(often described as the father of modern management)[1]

The starting point for this book is the notion that effective decision-making is the primary responsibility and *raison d'être* of management. This remains as true today as it has ever been. However, the way in which that responsibility might once have been understood has undergone an important transformation in recent years.

The traditional view of management was that, as Peter Drucker observed, 'only executives make decisions.' But what a growing number of companies are now realizing is that by restricting decision-making to just a few senior people in the organization they are limiting their effectiveness and the organization's ability to respond to new opportunities and threats. This realization is at the heart of much of the revolution in management practice over the past decade or so.

A management revolution

The revolution in management practice over the past few years has been characterized by a plethora of new and not so new management techniques and philosophies which have profoundly influenced the way that companies operate. Many of these – including business process re-engineering (BPR), total quality management (TQM) and,

> **'The starting point for this book is the notion that effective decision-making is the primary responsibility and *raison d'être* of management.'**

most obviously, the empowerment movement – have aimed at harnessing the intellect of workers further down the organization to tackle problems and, in many cases, to make decisions for themselves.

In some cases, the application of these techniques has greatly improved business performance. Where they have failed to produce results – and they have failed in many organizations – it is typically because decision-making power has not been pushed far enough down the organization.

All too often, for example, empowerment has meant giving people on the shopfloor responsibility for problems without the authority to tackle the issues at their root. In short, by failing to cascade their decision-making powers to those who can see what needs to be done, a great many managers – at all levels – have acted as blocks on change, which has meant that the anticipated benefits failed to materialize.

To some extent, this is a hangover from a time when information and holding the decision-making strings was viewed as a source of power which underpinned the management role. One thing that is clear, however, is that that style of management is no longer viable.

As Michael Hammer and James Champy observed in *Re-engineering the Corporation*, the book that triggered the business process re-engineering (BPR) movement:

> 'The costs of hierarchical decision-making are now too high to bear. Referring everything up the ladder means decisions get made too slowly for a fast-paced market.'[2]

In fact, today much of the progress being made in the sphere of management is about learning to let go – of both information and direct control. This is the essence of empowerment, but to date many of its implications have not been fully understood. In particular, the shift in the role of managers in the decision-making process from giving instructions or orders to facilitating effective decisions among others has been overlooked in many companies.

With luck, the ideas set out here may influence the decision-making habits of organizations and the people who run them. Above all else, though, this book is intended to be a practical guide to decision-making to help managers do their jobs more effectively.

Centralized and decentralized decision-making

The traditional argument put forward for limits on the decision-making power of managers and other employees is the need for control and consistency. How can a company maintain standards, the logic goes, if rules and operating procedures are constantly changing, and one hand doesn't know what the other is doing? The answer is that a balance is required between the freedom to make decisions at the appropriate level, and the control mechanisms to ensure that what happens in one part of the organization does not undermine it in other parts.

This is the classic tension between centralization and decentralization – or control and autonomy. It is an issue that companies have wrestled with for years. Indeed, in the post-war period many companies have been through a series of cycles, swinging from more centralized models to de-centralized models and back again as one or other became fashionable or new leadership demanded a different approach.

Better managed organizations tend to have less dramatic swings, but are also constantly tinkering, allowing managers in the field more freedom one year and reining them in the next.

As David Clutterbuck and Walter Goldsmith point out in their book *The Winning Streak Mark II*,[3] successful companies recognize the tension between control and autonomy and understand – albeit subconsciously – that small adjustments are required from time to time in order to strike the right balance. A recession may call for a tightening of spending controls from the centre, for example, requiring more decisions to be referred back. But when the economy picks up again, if those tighter controls on decision-making are not adjusted, then they can stifle entrepreneurship at the very moment the company needs to grow.

New styles of leadership

Other changes, too, are having an important impact on the way we understand the role of decision-makers. Most commentators would agree, for example, that the ability to make effective decisions is a core competence of leaders.

Today, however, by 'leaders' we don't just mean the chief executive or even senior managers. In today's organizations, anyone and everyone is a leader at some time in their work. Whether it is as the leader of the board of directors, a functional or departmental head, a team leader or simply the leader of their own work, each and every one of us is responsible for making our own decisions regarding our work or that of others around us.

Take the example of the woman working on an assembly line who sees a substandard product that has been allowed through by everyone else. In refusing to accept poor quality she is showing leadership – setting an example for others to follow. Her decision is that of a leader.

At the same time, the way we think about the role of management is also undergoing a transformation.

The changing role of management

A number of factors are forcing companies to look long and hard at how they can sustain competitive advantage in future. These include:

- the explosion of information technology

- the arrival of the knowledge worker
- an accelerating pace of change.

Underpinning many of these changes is a fundamental re-evaluation of the role of managers within organizations. Where once they were seen as the founts of all knowledge, with the knowhow to direct not just the efforts of others but the detail of how tasks were carried out, that is no longer the case. Today's managers are increasingly seen as 'facilitators', 'coaches' and 'enablers'.

The switch of emphasis is significant. Changes in the way that companies operate and the rise of so-called 'knowledge workers' in particular has meant that a typical manager may not know the detail of what someone in their team does. In future, too, they almost certainly won't have the skills to do that person's job. What this means in practice is that they are no longer able to tell the people who work for them what to do. Rather, their role is increasingly that of creating an environment in which others can apply their talents. There are good reasons for this.

The explosion of 'enabling' technology

Technology allows employees to communicate freely across the organization. It has the power to break down traditional hierarchies by enabling people at any level and any geographical location to talk to each other.

In more traditional companies, information technology (IT) is often used simply to duplicate the traditional hierarchy, with messages sent up the line to managers who then pass them on to their bosses or send them back down again to the person who will actually carry out the work. As such, the true potential of IT is not being realized in many organizations. But more progressive companies are already using IT to change the entire shape and structure of their decision-making processes.

The rise of the knowledge worker

Allied to the IT revolution is the arrival of the so-called 'knowledge worker' – individuals whose level of expertize often means they are beyond management direction. Commentators claim that the switch from physical work to intellectual work – 'brawn to brain' if you like – is already well under way in the more developed economies.

What have yet to be fully digested by many companies, however, are the implications for the way organizations are managed. As Thomas A Stewart points out in his book *Intellectual Capital: The New Wealth of Organizations*,[4] the arrival of the knowledge worker changes the role of managers, because the knowledge worker makes his or her own decisions.

As such, he says, the new 'knowledge economy' augurs the 'end of management as we know it'.

> *'The rise of the knowledge worker fundamentally alters the nature of work and the agenda of management. Managers are custodians; they protect and care for the assets of a corporation; when the assets are intellectual, the manager's job changes.'*

In essence, his argument is that the rise of knowledge workers means that the bosses no longer know more than the workers (if they ever really did). As a result, the logic of the management pyramid – a small number of people telling a large number of others what to do – is redundant.

In other words, today's knowledge workers carry the tools of their trade with them between their ears. It is they, and not their managers, who are the experts and must decide how to best deploy their knowhow. As a result,

> **'. . . the logic of the management pyramid . . . is redundant.'**

what they do has more in common with work carried out by people in the professions and must be assessed not by the tasks performed, but by the results achieved. Stewart says:

> *'A lawyer is not evaluated on the number of words in her closing argument but on how well-chosen and effective they are; not on the number of footnotes in her brief but on whether it makes a winning argument'.*

The lawyer doesn't have a boss telling her how to do her job – 'she has a client, a customer, who expects her to plan and organize her own work'. But, he might add, that client is totally unqualified to tell her how to do it, or make decisions that affect how she does it.

The enabling technology of IT is facilitating this change. As Bill Gates told Paul Taylor of the *Financial Times* recently: 'Companies want to empower their knowledge workers with information to make decisions. It is the lifeblood of a company.'[5]

Pace of change

The other point to realize is that if they want to be successful, companies really have no choice but to change the way they operate. Many commentators believe that the number one challenge facing business today is learning to live with ambiguity. In today's fast-moving business environment, threats and opportunities can come from almost anywhere, and the ability to cope with an uncertain future is the only competence that ensures success.

Moreover, the traditional basis for making decisions is increasingly fraught with danger. Western companies, in particular, have tended to base their decisions on the past. Today, however, that strategy is liable to land you in trouble. The reason is simply that the business environment is changing too fast and our ability to analyse data is too slow for us just to extrapolate lessons. In short, many markets don't stand still for long enough to get a useful fix.

One way to think about this is to say that decision-makers no longer have the luxury of taking aim at a stationary target. They have to be able to track a moving target and to aim slightly ahead to have any hope of hitting it.

Today, a number of relatively new techniques and ways of thinking are being used to help them do this. Ideas such as 'game theory', 'chaos theory' and 'scenario planning' are revolutionizing the way that managers approach decisions. By offering a more dynamic view of the world, they help us understand that decisions are not made in isolation from the real world of business, but are affected by the action and reaction of others. In so doing, they recognize that many of the old ways of looking at decisions are too mechanistic.

Mathematical formulae

In the past, many books concerned with decision-making have concentrated on mathematical formulae and probability theory. Indeed, decision science itself can be seen as an attempt to order the affairs of human beings. In some respects this is a worthy aim.

The problem for managers is that science, with its neat mathematical solutions, has little to do with the world in which they live. Their world, after all, is not black and white, but many shades of grey.

Moreover, the environment in which decisions are made is constantly changing and the speed of that change is accelerating. Above all else, though, the most important difference between the world managers live in and that explained by the mathematicians is that human beings, with all their hang-ups, prejudices, intuitions and other irrational ways, rarely conform with their idealized models.

As the linguistics expert Professor Noam Chomsky observed recently in *The Times*: 'As soon as questions of decision or reason or choice of action arise, human science is at a loss.' [6]

Central to this book, then, is the belief that decision-making is a fundamentally human activity. If we believe otherwise we might as well simply replace managers with computers, which are far better able to process information and make rational choices. In fact, it is precisely because decisions are made by human beings that they are so valuable to organizations.

In time, of course, advances in artificial intelligence and other types of technology may alter this situation. Even then it is doubtful whether a decision will ever truly be made without reference to the people who designed or programmed the machines. Furthermore, it can be argued that once you reduce decision-making to pure logic, then there is no decision to be made.

Inclusive management

A whole range of issues that are now on the business agenda place increasing emphasis on the decision-making process. One of the most important of these is the move to a more participative – or inclusive – management style.

This raises a whole series of other issues, including:

- how people and organizations learn
- what constitutes effective leadership
- the issue of stakeholders and who should have a say in the running of an organization
- the contribution of management and business to society at large
- corporate governance.

Closely allied to all these is the question of accountability. In the future these issues have important implications for the way that decisions are made – and the legitimacy of those decisions to stakeholders inside and outside of the organization.

Do we need managers at all?

It has been argued, by some commentators – Richard Koch and Ian Godden in their book *Managing Without Management*,[7] for example – that managers in the traditional sense have outstayed their usefulness.

'Something is wrong with our large corporations. For the first time ever, large firms are losing out to smaller ones. Nobody has explained why, or what to do about it. The early 1990s panaceas like empowerment and re-engineering are clearly incapable of stopping the rot. What has gone wrong with big business?'

Their explanation is simple: management has become a dead weight on business. Large corporations, they say, invented the concept of management as a necessary means of control and co-ordination. But in the second half of the century, 'managerial capitalism' mushroomed and has now become a costly leviathan, putting its own interests ahead of those of customers, investors and society in general. The solution? Get rid of it. Godden says:

> 'If you look at what management does at present, a large part of it is purely administrative. A typical manager's time is taken up with internal processes – paperwork, filing, writing letters and memos. Much of that has nothing to do with customers or the business, it is simply dealing with other managers.'

To some extent, this is true; although to say companies should get rid of managers is going too far. More accurately, what Koch and Godden are advocating is a fundamental re-evaluation of what management is there for. In particular, many of the tasks they have traditionally performed are no longer required. But other aspects of the role are now more important than ever.

In particular, managers have a vital role to play not only in ensuring that their own decisions are effective but also increasingly in facilitating effective decision-making among others.

The aim of this book, therefore, is to help practising managers to develop useful decision-making habits. In other words, it is concerned with understanding the behaviours – helpful and unhelpful – which underpin the decision-making process. As such, it is a holistic view of decision-making that is discussed here. The aim is that managers may gain a better understanding of their own mental models, and prejudices, to better direct their efforts in this crucial area of their work.

Taken together, what these factors add up to is the need for a fundamental shift in the way that decisions are viewed within organizations.

Drucker revisited

Taking all of these factors into account, we can re-frame Peter Drucker's famous quote for today's world as:

> 'The people who manage organizations do many things in addition to making decisions. But only people make decisions. The first managerial skill is, therefore, to ensure effective decisions are made.'

A route map to effective decision-making

This book aims to set out a route map for effective decision-making, with successive chapters exploring the key steps.

1. Understanding what decisions are, the sorts of decisions that managers have to make, and the reasons for ineffective decision-making.

2. An outline of some of the models which provide a conceptual framework for the way we think about decisions.

3. A basic tool-kit for decision-makers.

4. The time-scales involved.

5. Obtaining and interrogating the information on which decisions are based.

6. The sorts of organizational structures which help and hinder effective decision-making.

7. The way that culture – organizational and national – can affect the outcome of a decision.

8. The role of soft skills such as intuition.

9. The ethical dimension of business decisions.

10. Putting it all together and implementing it.

Along the way, the book is intended to stimulate thought and uncover some of the hidden issues which so often affect the outcome of decisions.

References

1. Drucker, Peter, *Management*, Pan, 1979.

2. Hammer, Michael, and Champy, James, *Re-engineering the Corporation*, p 96, Nicholas Brealey, 1993.

3. Clutterbuck, David, and Goldsmith, Walter, *The Winning Streak Mark II*, Orion, 1997.

4. Stewart, Thomas A, *Intellectual Capital: The new wealth of organizations*, Nicholas Brealey, 1997.

5. Taylor, Paul, 'Computer, read my lips', *Financial Times*, 11 November 1996.

6. Finn, Widget, 'Cutting out the indecision', *The Times*, 12 September 1996.

7. Koch, Richard, and Godden, Ian, *Managing Without Management*, Nicholas Brealey, 1996.

Decisions, decisions, decisions

'The souls of men of undecided and feeble purpose are the graveyards of good intentions.'
UNKNOWN

From the moment we wake up to the moment our heads hit the pillow again (and sometimes even after), our brains buzz with an endless stream of decisions affecting our personal and professional lives. They range from the trivial issues that confront each one of us on a daily basis – which tie or shirt to wear to work, whether to drive or take the train – to more serious considerations – whether to take the new job we've been offered or stay put; whether to retrain for a different career altogether.

Once at our desks, the daily round of decisions continues as we shuffle paper and e-mails from in-trays to out-trays at a head-spinning rate. It has been estimated that the typical Western manager makes literally hundreds of decisions each day of varying significance. Given that statistic, it is surprising that we aren't better at making decisions than we are.

Writing in *The Times* recently, management journalist Widget Finn observed:

> *'On average managers attend six meetings a week, and according to a recent BT survey up to 80 per cent of those meetings are considered unproductive. Nearly one day in five, or two months of the working year are spent meeting other people and coming to no particular conclusion. No doubt someone soon will work out the annual cost of indecision to British business.'*[1]

If they did, they would discover that the cost is staggering: perhaps then companies would recognize the importance of effective decision-making habits. The fact is that very few of us have any sort of formal training in this area. That is not to say that we do not perceive ourselves as good decision-makers (even though many of us are not), or that we lack the knowledge to make informed choices. Rather, it is the result of the simple fact that organizations do not recognize decision-making as an explicit skill that can be learned.

'... the typical Western manager makes literally hundreds of decisions each day of varying significance.'

This is a great shame because, as this book sets out to demonstrate, effective decision-making strategies can be acquired just like any other useful behaviour or discipline. What makes the current situation all the more regrettable is that decisions are the bread and butter of management.

First, however, it is necessary to understand a little more about the nature of decisions.

WHAT ARE DECISIONS?

A decision is the point at which a choice is made between alternative – and usually competing – options. As such, it may be seen as a stepping-off point – the moment at which a commitment is made to one course of action to the exclusion of others. In practice, it is the commitment made to a particular course of action that imbues a decision with significance.

It is no coincidence that the word 'decision' actually comes from a word which means 'to cut', or as Helga Drummond says in her book *Effective Decision-making*, 'to resolve upon a specific choice or course of action'.[2]

Drummond makes an important distinction between a decision *per se*, and the decision-making process. The decision, she suggests, is the final outcome of the process, but the decision-making process involves 'events leading up to the moment of choice and beyond'.

This is a valid point. However, as with so many processes which take place in the human brain, it is difficult – if not impossible – to entirely separate cause from effect here.

Moreover, as Alan Barker points out:

> *'Making a decision is more than choosing what to do. It involves making a commitment, however small: rationally and emotionally. Furthermore, it often involves making a commitment on behalf of others – particularly in a work or family situation – and asking them to commit to your commitment.'*[3]

A crossroads in the forest

An analogy may help to clarify these points. A group of travellers, on approaching a particularly hazardous forest, hire a guide to show them the way. In so doing they vest decision-making power in the guide.

After a while the party reaches a crossroads. In this situation, it is not simply that the guide (the decision-maker) favours one road over another that matters, it is that the travellers will act on his decision.

There may be more than one path leading out of the forest, for example. So, although the guide may pause to consider the best path, the significance of the decision is that once it is made, for good or ill, the journey will continue in that direction. If the journey is a particularly hard one, it may be, too, that it is the resolve with which the travellers set out, rather than the path chosen, that will ultimately determine the success of the enterprise.

This analogy also illustrates another important point touched on earlier. There is a distinction between the guide's decision, and the process by which he arrives at it. The decision is the outcome of the decision-making process, but they are not the same thing.

For example, if the guide knows the forest well there may be many points that he takes into consideration before reaching his decision about the best path to take – how much water the party is able to carry, and the likelihood of meeting wild animals. On the other hand, he may use a different process. Imagine that he is hopelessly lost and when no-one is looking flips a coin to determine which road to take. Either way, once the decision is made, he commits the party to that course of action.

Inputs and outputs

The concept of 'process' is now widely understood by managers, so the distinction between the process by which decisions are made and the decisions themselves should be clear.

In this context, final decisions can be seen as the outputs, and data, opinions and other ingredients that influence the decision can be seen as inputs. This is something we will return to in a later chapter.

To recap then, the decision-making process involves what Drummond calls 'events leading up to the moment of choice and beyond'. But, once it is made, the decision itself always involves what Alan Barker calls a 'point of no return'.

THE POINT OF NO RETURN

The point of no return is the stage at which the decision-maker commits himself to a certain course of action – thereby making the decision. Before the point of no return is reached it is possible to turn back, but once it has been passed a commitment is made.

This is the case, Barker argues, even with decisions that involve a number of stepping-off points, such as a project. Typically, the costs of a change of mind will rise as each successive point is passed, until it becomes impossible to contemplate a U-turn, even though it may be difficult to identify exactly when the point of no return was reached.

The existence of the point of no return in decision-makers' minds is at the root of many disastrous decisions. This is compounded by the fact that organizations, because of their nature, are especially vulnerable to the effects of something called 'groupthink' which is discussed in Chapter 7. But for now, let us look at different ways of categorizing decisions.

DIFFERENT TYPES OF DECISIONS

In general, this book is about business decisions – that is the sorts of decisions people are likely to encounter in their working lives. Within that broad definition, however, the academic literature defines two different types of decisions:

1. operational decisions
2. strategic decisions.

Operational decisions are concerned with the day-to-day running of the business. Typical operational decisions might involve setting production levels, the decision to recruit additional employees, or to close a particular factory.

Strategic decisions are those concerned with organizational policy and direction over a longer time period. So, a strategic decision might involve determining whether to enter a new market, acquire a competitor or exit from an industry altogether.

Interestingly, Madan G Singh, chair of information engineering at Manchester Institute of Science and Technology, and an acknowledged expert on decision-making, prefers breakdown of decision levels, which recognizes some of the changes taking place within companies.

In a recent interview with the Internet magazine *Exec!*[4] he divides decision in an organization into three levels:

- day-to-day decisions
- tactical decisions
- strategic decisions.

Day-to-day decisions, he says, are those made by front-line staff. Collectively, they make thousands of decisions daily, most of them in a short time-frame and on the basis of concrete information – answering a customer's request for information about a product, for example. Their decisions usually have a narrow scope and influence a small range of activities.

Tactical and strategic decisions, on the other hand, are both longer-term decisions. The data needed to make them is much broader, extending outside the organization, and the information derived from that data is less precise, less current and subject to more error.

Tactical decisions, Singh says, cover a few weeks to a few months, and include decisions such as the pricing of goods and services, and deciding advertising and marketing expenditures.

Strategic decisions are those with the longest time horizon – one to five years or longer. They generally concern expanding or contracting the business or entering new geographic or product markets.

There are other ways of categorizing decisions. One obvious method takes account of how significant they are to the organization – or the size of their potential impact. On these lines, it is possible to view decisions as small, medium or large.

Exactly what constitutes a big decision will depend on the size and nature of the business. For example, for a small firm an investment of £50,000 might be a big decision, while for a multinational it would be no more than a drop in the ocean. (On the other hand, the same investment may represent a big decision for a very junior manager, even though its impact on the organization is limited to his or her immediate career prospects).

The general principle holds, however, that some decisions are of a greater magnitude than others. Take the example of the marketing department of a food manufacturer. A series of decisions escalating in size might look something like this:

- **small decision** – the decision to make a minor change to the packaging of an existing product (operational decision);
- **medium decision** – the decision to launch a new product in an existing range (operational decision, but with potential implications for strategy);
- **large decision** – the decision to enter a new market (strategic decision).

By understanding the magnitude of a decision, it is possible to determine the resources that should be allocated to it. What many managers fail to realize, however, is that time – whether their own or someone else's – is often the most scarce resource of all.

Money or people decisions?

Another useful categorization for decisions is offered by the American writer and public speaker Roger Dawson.[5] Decisions, he says, can be thought of as either:

- money decisions
- people decisions.

By understanding which type of decision a manager is dealing with, Dawson says, it is possible to arrive at a more effective solution. The problem, however, is that if they are not thought through, the two can easily be confused.

For example, a valuable manager who threatens to leave the company unless he receives a big salary increase poses a dilemma to the organization. But it is only by assessing the cause and impact of the ultimatum that an effective decision will be arrived at.

The decision-maker needs to probe underneath the surface to uncover the issues. On the surface it appears to be a money decision. But is it a question of money, or is it a case of a manager who feels stifled in his job and wants to feel valued? If the former, then it can best be handled by hard-nosed negotiation, but the latter requires a lighter touch and perhaps a creative solution, such as giving the individual a challenging new role.

HOW DECISIONS ARE MADE (in theory)

There is a whole academic discipline devoted to understanding management decision-making. Much of it is built on the foundations set down by economists in the early industrial period, who believed that under a given set of circumstances human behaviour was logical and therefore predictable. Using this premise, they built models to explain the workings of commerce which they believed could be extended to the way in which decisions were made.

> 'The decision-maker needs to probe underneath the surface to uncover the issues.'

Such models rest on a number of assumptions about the way in which economic agents – the people who manage companies, for instance – will behave when confronted with a set of circumstances.

First and foremost among these was an assumption that agents act rationally: in other words, that given accurate information, they will arrive at a logical conclusion about the decision most likely to produce the desired result. Another important assumption was that business decisions are driven by the desire to maximize profits.

These assumptions allowed mathematicians to derive formulae – based on probability theory – which offered managers useful decision-making tools. At its crudest, for example, simple cost-benefit analysis was supposed to help managers evaluate different options. However, theory and practice are rarely the same thing.

This is not surprising. Underpinning this mathematical approach are a number of flawed assumptions. For example, it assumes that the decision-making process managers rely on is:

1. consistent
2. based on accurate information
3. free from emotion or prejudice
4. rational.

We know better.

Yet the idea of rational decision-making persists. Even today, it is argued that effective decision-making involves a number of logical steps. This is often referred to as the 'rational model of decision-making' or the 'synoptic model'.

The synoptic model

The synoptic model involves the following steps:

1. Identify problem.
2. Clarify problem and prioritize goals.
3. Generate options.
4. Evaluate options (using appropriate analysis).
5. Compare predicted outcomes of each option with goals.
6. Choose option which best matches goals.

It should be said at this point that the synoptic model is very much a Western model (the way in which Eastern cultures such as the Japanese and Koreans understand decision-making is very different and is examined in Chapter 7 of this book).

The problem with the synoptic model is that, although it provides a logical explanation of how decisions might be made, our own experience tells us that this is not actually what happens. (Nor, some would argue, is it even desirable.)

THE HUMAN FACTOR

'No-one knows what goes through a decision-maker's head at the moment of choice,' John F Kennedy once observed. As he was someone who himself took some big decisions – including those during the Cuban Missile Crisis which took the world to the brink of a Third World War, and others which paved the way to putting the first man on the moon – his words have special significance. They suggest that even the one making the decision does not fully comprehend the factors or mental processes involved.

Perhaps we would prefer to think of leaders as clear-sighted decision-makers, but most of us can empathize with the sentiment expressed by Kennedy. We simply do not know why we make the decisions we do.

Often, we end up rationalizing the decision after it has been made, even though deep down we know that the reasons given are not those which swayed the balance. Admitting this in no way takes away from the decisions each of us makes, nor does it necessarily make them any easier. But it does at least open the door to a more useful understanding of what makes us tick as decision-makers.

That said, it is not the intention of this book to dismiss decision science; far from it. Rather, what this book seeks to do is to set decision-making in its human context: in other words, to understand the imperfections and faults that can all too easily lead to poor judgement and bad decisions.

HOW ARE DECISIONS REALLY MADE?

The point about the human factor also goes a long way towards explaining why so many bad decisions are made. Viewed in this way, the answer would seem to be because human beings are fallible – they make mistakes. In reality, however, the picture is much more complicated.

For one thing, we all know that it is entirely possible to make the right decision for all the wrong reasons. You might decide on a course of action, the logic of which is contradicted by the available data, only to find that the context suddenly changes and the decision yields a successful outcome.

A useful example here is the decision to buy shares. This can be used to illustrate a number of points: for example, a decision to buy shares in a company with poor past performance could be a brilliant one if future performance bears no relationship to the past. But the opposite is also true: it is equally plausible to make the wrong decision for all the right reasons. So buying shares in a company which has consistently outperformed its competitors looks a good bet until the company falls on its face. (The issue of intuition is dealt with more fully in Chapter 8.)

Works for me

The corollary to this is that what makes a decision work for one person may be the very factor that eliminates it for another. In both cases, too, the final decision may be the right one if there is sufficient commitment to see it through. The opposite is also true: many sound decisions result in failure because the organization lacks the resolve to make them work. It is useful to bear this in mind when making decisions.

One of the issues an effective decision-maker will consider is the level of commitment within the organization to a particular course of action. The point here is that a decision may be brilliant in its conception, but fail simply because others are not committed to it.

AN ART, NOT A SCIENCE

The reality is that decision-making is an art not a science. Effective decision-makers realize this and balance a number of elements. These include the need for hard data and rigorous analysis, but also softer less tangible aspects such as intuition, experience, and moral and ethical judgements.

To view decision-making as a hard discipline is to miss the subtleties of the art. One way to think about this is to consider logic, intuition and experience as three sides of the decision triangle.

The decision-making triangle

Effective decision-making involves balancing three elements: logic, intuition and experience. Each of these has a bearing on the way we understand the issues involved and reach our conclusions.

The triangle in Figure 1.1, for example, represents a decision where all three elements are equally balanced. However, in practice, the emphasis will vary according to the decision-making style of the individual or group, and the type of decision to be made. The interplay of these factors will determine the shape of the triangle.

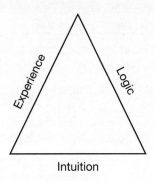

Figure 1.1 The decision-making triangle

21

Figure 1.2 Decision-making triangle showing decision-making style

So, for example, the decision-making style of someone who relies very heavily on logic, and to a lesser extent their own experience, but puts little store in intuition could be represented as shown in Figure 1.2.

Mixing and matching decision triangles

It is possible to think of effective decision-making as a good match between the shape of the decision and the decision-making style or approach applied to it. The trick to good decision-making habits, then, lies in:

- understanding your own style (your natural triangle)
- recognizing the shape of a particular decision (its unique triangle)
- as far as possible, compensating to match the two.

Neat as this is, however, it is far too mechanistic an approach to have much validity in the real world. Its chief value is as a conceptual tool to understand why some people are good at some decisions and lousy at others.

By varying the mix of the three key elements, it is possible to alter the way we view decisions, and open up new vistas.

As Elspeth McFadzeon, an expert on decision-making and lecturer at Henley Management College explains:

'Creativity is enhanced when experience and ideas are mixed together and transformed. The key is to introduce new pieces to the puzzle to create new relationships among the existing elements. Mix up how you think about things, and you'll find that the boundary of the problem is completely destroyed.'

Challenging as this is, many managers would prefer it if decisions came in neat little boxes. The trouble is that business life is not that simple.

Such an individual will have a clear advantage when tackling decisions which require this balance – for example, whether to locate a factory on a particular site – but will be at a disadvantage in a situation requiring a more intuitive approach – deciding what to do about a manager whose previously excellent performance is suffering as a result of problems at home, or even spotting a paradigm shift in his industry. (We will return to the decision-making triangle in Chapter 8.)

Try drawing a triangle for your own decision-making style. Now ask colleagues to draw your decision-making style. How closely do the two match?

Why are bad decisions made?

There are numerous factors that can cause a decision to go awry. However, there are some common factors which frequently contribute to bad decisions. These include:

- poor match between the decision and the decision-making style of those involved
- failure to spot the root problem or recognize the real issue
- problem incorrectly defined or expressed in the wrong terms
- failure to change course or revoke an earlier bad decision (groupthink)
- inaccurate or incomplete information
- personal bias, prejudice or dishonesty
- arrogance
- complacency
- decision delayed until too late (reactive rather than proactive stance)
- fear – of the consequences of making a decision
- cowardice
- problem ignored or hidden (ignorance)
- decision made at wrong level (inappropriate decision-maker)
- failure to follow through (lack of commitment)
- apathy (lack of will)
- anarchy (lack of discipline)
- unforeseen circumstances (surprise)
- paradigm shift (the world changes)
- poor implementation (lack of leadership)

23

- failure to think it through (sloppy decision-making)
- panic
- laziness
- inexperience
- lack of resources
- inadequate training or preparation
- poor judgement
- lack of confidence (poor credibility to self or others).

The list goes on. But one other factor merits special attention.

Fighting the last war

This term is applied to situations where the solutions to yesterday's problems are employed to solve those faced today.

Often, but not always, this mistake is associated with too much rather than too little experience. If someone has experienced a problem before they are more likely to see a parallel with a current problem even though the context may have changed. By contrast, a fresh pair of eyes will be more likely to see the problem for what it is.

In truth, most organizations have a bias towards basing decisions on the past. Quite simply, because we can't predict the future, our desire for empirical evidence to validate a course of action leads us to apply lessons from the past to current situations. To some extent unless we are prepared to throw caution to the wind – as sometimes we must – we will always base decisions on the last cycle of events, or on extrapolations of it.

This is because we:

1. crave data to validate decisions (we are data junkies)

2. are unable to predict the future.

To resolve the problem, it is much easier to get our 'data fix' from what happened before.

This can be a particular problem for senior managers, who, because of their broad experience, have a tendency to base decisions on the way things worked when they were hands-on managers. As a result, in the event of a new paradigm – i.e., a fundamental change one day – they may be wrong-footed.

Classic examples include IBM, which failed to fully appreciate the significance of the move to PCs and the impact it would have on the mainframe business. Interestingly, one theory (and there are lots) about what went wrong when IBM was first considering how best to move into the PC market, is that the managers in charge of the project short-circuited the normal decision-making process in order to get an IBM-badged machine into the market quickly.

This theory suggests that far from blinkering the organization as some commentators have suggested, the famous 'IBM way' if followed might have ensured the organization had a much tighter control on the technology, either owning it outright or establishing an exclusive licensing arrangement. However, rather than handle the negotiations for the DOS operating system in the normal way, which would have involved a much more thorough exploration of these sorts of issues, short cuts in the decision-making process allowed Bill Gates to retain control. The rest, as they say, is history.

And Big Blue wasn't the only company to be caught out by the paradigm shift. As Tony Hodgson, managing director of Idon Associates,[6] a consultancy based in Scotland, observes:

> *'Back in the 1970s, the head of Digital Equipment asked why anyone in their right mind would want a computer on their desk. This man was a visionary in his day, but the game had moved on. It's so easy to get beached as time moves on.'*

Just how the strategists sitting in their offices far removed from where the action is can identify and react to changes in the marketplace is a theme covered in Chapter 8. For now, suffice it to say that, as with many other aspects of the decision-making process, once we have understood the in-built bias and allowed for it in our calculations the tendency to fight the last war is not nearly the problem it might at first seem.

Knowing that we have a tendency to look backwards when we try to predict the future affords us some protection from its negative effects.

Leave the baggage at the station

One company which has been highly successful in riding the currents of change is Reuters, the financial information and news company. Chief executive Peter Job explained a key factor during an interview for *The Winning Streak Mark II*.[7]

Asked how the company balanced its long-term strategy with the need for urgency in a fast-moving market, Job replied:

> *'I think our board has a very clear understanding that every now and then changes occur which could be significant. You have to watch out for those changes. In the US they describe it as a new paradigm. The Internet, for example could be a new paradigm. At those times it's important to leave your strategy suitcase in the station and catch the train.'*

By this, he means that, faced with major change, senior managers must be prepared to abandon their long-term strategic decisions or risk being left behind.

CASE STUDY: HONDA

In *Managing on the Edge*, Richard Pascale[8] recounts the story of how Honda decided to launch its motorcycles into Los Angeles, as part of a grand strategy to break into the US market.

The company sent some people to California expecting to promote its larger, more powerful bikes. In order to get around town, the sales team used some of the newly developed small 50cc bikes. These attracted a lot of attention wherever they went, Eventually, the sales people started receiving inquiries, not from motorcycle dealers but from sports shops and other retailers. It seemed that fewer people were interested in the large machines.

Contrary to the expectations of Mr Honda and his advisers in America, the 50cc bikes were to become the biggest seller. They opened up the US market to Honda, and within four years Honda was marketing almost 50 per cent of all motorcycles sold in the USA.

The significant factor in this story is the readiness of Honda's managers to leave the strategy baggage in the station and climb aboard the train. There are a number of reasons for this. For one thing, the team in America did not call back to Tokyo to say that (as Toyota had previously found) the strategy for launching the more powerful machines was failing. Instead, they offered the alternative idea that the market was crying out for the smaller machines.

Moreover, the fact that the company had expended a lot of effort deciding on and putting together a strategy to sell a product into a major market did not prevent it from switching to a different strategy to take advantage of the opportunity presented. even though a variety of alternative actions might have been taken: the sales people could have been fired for incompetence because they had failed to sell the larger bikes, for example; or a different sales strategy involving a heavy investment in advertising could have been adopted.

Instead, Honda's senior management abandoned their hard-fought-for strategy on account of the judgement of a few relatively junior employees several thousand miles away in an as yet unproven market.

WHY DECISIONS ARE NOT MADE

It is true to say, too, that for every mistake that results from a wrong decision there is another caused by the failure to make any decision at all. This can all too easily result in one of three effects.

1. **An opportunity is missed.**
2. **Corrective or evasive action is not taken in time to avert a serious problem.**
3. **Other parts of the organization are paralyzed and unable to do their jobs properly.**

Any one of which can lead to a crisis. Unfortunately, there is a tendency for people to assume that by not making a decision they are leaving their options open. This is usually not true.

A decision-maker – like a parachutist over the designated drop-zone – has a window of opportunity in which to hit the target. That window may last days, months or years but it will pass. It may last only minutes or seconds – a fact that is well understood by City traders who have to make snap decisions, often with millions of pounds riding on their judgements. For them, a delay of even a few seconds can mean an opportunity is lost or a potential threat becomes an expensive reality.

Factors which prevent decisions from being made

The question of making decisions in appropriate time-scales is one to which we will return in Chapter 4. For now, suffice it to say that there are several factors that prevent decisions being made. Among them are:

- unwillingness to grasp the nettle.
- failure to recognize a problem in time
- procrastination
- failure to identify a paradigm shift
- preoccupation with other day-to-day problems – (too busy fire-fighting)
- internal politics
- lack of will (apathy or poor leadership)
- lack of urgency (poor leadership or lack of resources)
- corporate myopia

▶

▶

- weak reporting lines
- inadequate data
- too much data
- failure to delegate (lack of empowerment)
- incompetence
- dithering (indecisiveness)
- too many people involved in decision-making process (management by committee)
- decisions given low priority.
- a decision-making bottleneck in the organization.

The last situation in particular merits special consideration: as Figure 1.3 suggests, a manager who procrastinates over decisions creates a bottleneck in the organization which prevents others, including front-line employees, and managers in other departments from getting on with their jobs.

Opening doors with facilitating decisions

Facilitating decisions are those which enable others to function more effectively. Typically they involve removing obstacles from the paths of employees further down the organization.

One of the most significant changes that has taken place in recent years is an increase in the discretionary powers companies give to the employees closest to the customer. In light of this, it is becoming increasingly important for managers to recognize facilitating decisions which clear obstacles from the paths of those entrusted with these new decision-making and problem-solving powers.

An analogy that can be applied to decision-making in organizations is that of managers as key keepers, where keys represent decision-making powers. What happens in all too many organizations is that employees are

'... it is becoming increasingly important for managers to recognize facilitating decisions ...'

unable to work effectively because doors are locked to them and they are not given the keys to unlock them.

How many times, for example, have you heard an employee complain that they are unable to get into a storeroom, warehouse or filing

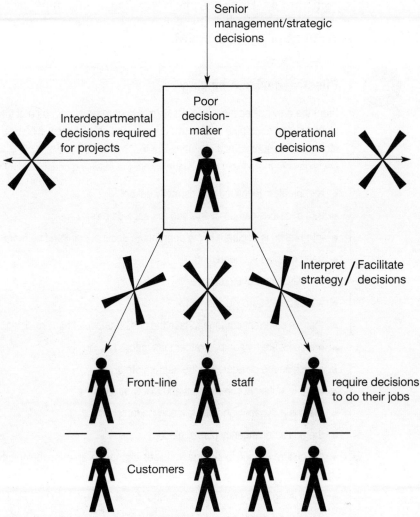

Figure 1.3 Decision-making bottleneck

cabinet to retrieve information they need to do their job because the manager is the only person trusted with the key? This is all the more frustrating when the problem occurs when the manager is not around.

By the same token, many organizations restrict the ability of their employees to open the necessary doors (i.e., make appropriate decisions) by refusing to trust them with the authority to do so.

There are good reasons, you might argue, for not allowing every Tom, Dick and Harry to make their own decisions – not least the need to maintain standards, or where there are safety concerns or other legal considerations. However, those decisions which must be made by a manager who is accountable can often be made in advance, so that in effect the door is kept unlocked.

Effective decision-making

From the previous sections it is possible to generalize about some of the elements that contribute to effective decision-making. These will be dealt with in more detail in subsequent chapters. But for now we can say that effective decisions are more likely to be made where the following conditions are met:

- root problem identified and correctly defined
- bad decisions can be overturned (no sacred cows)
- information is accurate to the appropriate decimal point and no more
- personal bias is understood
- humility is part of the culture
- a proactive stance is adopted
- there is sufficient courage to face the consequences of any decision
- problems are faced up to rather than ignored
- decisions are delegated to the appropriate level
- there is sufficient commitment and follow through
- there is a dynamic and disciplined workforce
- there is a contingency plan in place
- the culture is open to change and sees change as an opportunity rather than a threat
- there is vigorous implementation (strong leadership)
- decisions are thought-out.

And where decision-makers are:

- cool under fire (good crisis management)
- energetic
- have relevant experience
- provided with adequate resources
- given adequate training and preparation
- confident (high credibility with self and others)

▶

- aware of tendency to fight the last war
- competent
- able to build consensus when required.

And are supported with:

- sufficient data (at the right level of detail)
- authority as well as responsibility (strong empowerment).

This is best achieved where organizations are:

- willing to grasp the nettle and root out problems before they become a serious threat
- action-oriented
- able to look ahead, and make space for strategy and planning
- focused on external world (customer /competitors, for example, rather than internal politics)
- strong-willed (strong leadership)
- able to create a sense of urgency and energy.

And where:

- there are strong reporting lines.
- decision-making is given high priority.

To this, two earlier points should be added:

- decision-making is an art not a science
- sometimes, almost any decision is better than no decision.

LUCKY GENERALS

Finally in this chapter, a word about that most elusive of all management competencies – luck.

It was Napoleon who said that his most important asset was lucky generals. It is striking, too, how often his words are echoed by captains of industry. In a series of interviews for the book *The Winning Streak Mark II*, this theme recurred again and again.

The book set out to explore whether there were key factors in the style of management that were common to companies that had been successful over a long period. As part of the research team, I helped interview chief executives and chairmen from some of the world's leading companies. To cut a long story short, we concluded that there were indeed common characteristics in the way these companies were managed. But the word 'luck', too, was mentioned many times.

The top management of one of our companies in particular referred again and again to the important role luck had played in the success of the business: being in the right place at the right time. What is surprising perhaps is that the company was Reuters, one the most technologically sophisticated organizations in the world.

14 tips for decision-making

In their book *Smart Moves for People in Charge*, the American management authors Sam Deep and Lyle Sussman offer 14 useful tips for decision-making.[9] They are as follows:

- Recognize your personal decision-making biases. Are you emotional or logical? Fast-acting or deliberative?
- Open your ears and mind to perspectives different from your own.
- Fight the temptation to solve today's problem with yesterday's solution.
- Solve problems with a win–win orientation.
- Solicit information from the individuals affected by the decision.
- Make sure you're solving the right problem. Look between the problem and the solution to understand its nature.
- Consider as many solutions as possible.
- Realize that even the best solutions may open the door to new problems.
- If you're using 'hard data' as the basis for your decision, verify the numbers. Remember, numbers crunched by humans with opinions are inherently biased.
- When making decisions that affect others, share the reasoning behind the decision.
- Think in terms of 'satisficing', not optimizing. The satisficing decision-maker recognizes that there is no such thing as the best choice; only good and poor choices. Choose accordingly.
- Ask a lot of questions.
- Learn from prior decisions.
- Ask for criticism. Keep people around you who are strong enough to challenge your ideas so bad ones never make it out of the office.

References

1. Finn, Widget, 'Cutting out the indecision', *The Times*, 12 September 1996

2. Drummond, Helga, *Effective Decision-making*, 2nd edition, Kogan Page, 1996.

3. Barker, Alan, *How to be a Better Decision-maker*, Kogan Page, 1996.

4. *Exec!* Home Page, 17 June 1997.

5. Dawson, Roger, *Make the Right Decision Every Time*, Nicholas Brealey, 1994.

6. Dearlove, Des, 'Just imagine', *Human Resources*, July 1997.

7. Clutterbuck, David, and Goldsmith, Walter, *The Winning Streak Mark II*, Orion, 1997.

8. Pascale, Richard, *Managing on the Edge*, Simon & Schuster, New York, 1990.

9. Deep, Sam, and Sussman, Lyle, *Smart Moves for People in Charge*, Addison-Wesley, 1995.

2

The garbage can and other models

'*When desperate ills demand a speedy cure, distrust is cowardice, and prudence folly.*'
SAMUEL JOHNSON

'*Perfection is the enemy of effectiveness. An effective plan executed now is better than a perfect plan executed next quarter or next year.*'
DONALD G KRAUSE, *The Way of the Leader*

Having said at the outset that this book is intended to be a practical aid to decision-makers, it is with some trepidation that we dip our toes into decision theory. The fact is, however, that a rudimentary understanding of some of the models which underpin the way we think about decisions is both useful and illuminating.

Here, we consider:

- the garbage can model
- the rational deductive model
- disjointed incrementalism
- reductionism
- scientific management – Taylorism
- universal predictability
- total quality management (TQM)
- chaos theory
- game theory.

(This is by no means an exhaustive list.)

Some of the more general business models that have been developed to help managers understand the way that organizations function and to formulate strategy also offer useful decision-making frameworks. These include Porter's Five Competitive Forces and the Boston matrix, which are both considered in Chapter 3.

This chapter, however, aims to put the decision-making process into some sort of theoretical context. Besides, some of the models have such great names!

> 'This chapter . . . aims to put the decision-making process into some sort of theoretical context.'

THE GARBAGE CAN MODEL

This is the name given to a pattern of decision-making in organizations first identified by the American Professor of Management James March. In simple terms, it describes an organizational model where, when faced with a decision, members of the organization generate a constant stream of problems and solutions. These are then in effect 'dumped' into a 'garbage can', and only a very small percentage of the solutions generated are ever incorporated in the final decision.

Underpinning this model are Professor March's observations[1] on organizational behaviour, which suggest that the people working in organizations tend to develop a preference for certain courses of action. These may be regarded as the 'pet solutions' of their individual champions. The upshot of this, the model implies, is that whenever a problem arises, individuals will seize upon it as an opportunity to implement their chosen solution. This in turn influences both the decision-making process and the final output.

Another way to look at this model is to see organizations as sets of competing solutions waiting for problems to arise. Under the garbage can model, then, decisions can be regarded as what happens when a set of problems, solutions and choices come together – or collide – at a particular juncture. In a sense, the final decision is no more than the by-product of the alchemy that takes place within the garbage can.

(This fits with another idea put forward by March and another American management academic Richard Cyert, which sees the way organizations behaved as a form of 'organized anarchy'.)

THE RATIONAL DEDUCTIVE MODEL

At the other end of the spectrum is the rational deductive model of decision-making. In essence, this is the 'rational model' or 'synoptic model' of decision-making' referred to in Chapter 1. It merits a second mention here under its more scientific name for two reasons. First, it is probably the best-known model – or theory – of how decisions are made (although it is certainly not the most accurate). Second, it provides a useful counterpoint to the next model, disjointed incrementalism.

To recap, the synoptic model suggests that decision-makers follow a number of steps. These are:

1. Identify problem.
2. Clarify problem and prioritize goals.
3. Generate options.
4. Evaluate options (using appropriate analysis).
5. Compare predicted outcomes of each option with goals.
6. Choose option which best matches goals.

Although not explicitly so, there is an implication with this model that decision-makers are able to foresee what will occur as a result of the decision they make. This is an important distinction between it and the next model.

DISJOINTED INCREMENTALISM

This is the name given to a pattern of decision-making in organizations which was identified by another American academic – the political scientist Charles Lindblom. Lindblom concluded that most decisions are taken piecemeal as the problem unfolds, with each decision having little reference to the previous ones.

To some extent, disjointed incrementalism is the 'we'll cross that bridge when we get to it' school of decision-making. Frankly, it has much to recommend it to the practical-minded. Why after all waste a great deal of time and energy pondering decisions that may or may not have to be made further down the road?

This differs sharply from the rational deductive model – which suggests that a problem can be fully identified and understood at the outset, and relevant information collected in order to set out the options which can then be assessed rationally before the most appropriate course of action is chosen.

Lindblom believed that disjointed incrementalism was actually a much more sensible way to approach decision-making. This is because the human capacity to absorb information is limited, and even if it were possible to identify which information was relevant at the outset, perfect information is rarely available.

In short, Lindblom, at least, knew that he was dealing with human beings. He also understood that it is better to deal with the way things really are than to imagine perfect knowledge.

One other point before leaving this model. There is another important advantage it offers as a decision-making framework. By explicitly assuming that each decision is separate from the last, it frees managers from their previous mistakes.

The point here is that if the decision-makers' hands are not tied by what has gone before, then they are more likely to base each new decision on what is happening now rather than what happened yesterday or a year ago.

REDUCTIONISM

More than just a model, reductionism is a scientific movement that has had a great influence on the way we think about problems. This approach is based on the belief that if a problem can be reduced to its smallest component and that component understood, then it is possible to comprehend the whole.

Scientists in particular believed for a time that if they could understand how the smallest particle in the universe worked, then they would unlock all its other secrets. The problem that dogged them, however, was that every time they thought they had successfully identified the smallest particle of matter, someone came up with an even smaller one. At one point, they believed that the atom was the smallest element. Now they just don't know.

It seems unlikely that we are any more able to understand the smallest components of the universe than we are the whole, and, as a consequence, reductionism as a model has taken a bit of a battering in recent years. Yet its fingerprints can still be seen on much of the management literature that has been produced this century.

SCIENTIFIC MANAGEMENT: TAYLORISM

The application of reductionism in the world of management can perhaps best be seen in the work of Frederick Winslow Taylor.[2] Although now largely disregarded, Taylor's ideas actually underpin a great deal of management thinking and decision-making today.

Taylor was an industrial engineer whose ideas, developed at the turn of the century, became known as 'scientific management'. Famous for his time and motion studies at the Midvale Steel Works, where he was chief engineer, he used his stopwatch to break down complex processes into simple tasks, thereby increasing efficiency.

As management writer Stuart Crainer explains:

'Taylor's "science" came from the minute examination of individual workers' tasks. Having identified every single movement and action involved in performing a task, Taylor believed he could determine the optimum time required to complete it. Armed with this information, a manager could decide whether a worker was doing the job well.'[3]

However, Taylor saw the way that management organized labour as the limit of decision-making within an organization. In effect, he saw workers as nothing more than the components in a machine which was operated by management.

Today, happily, workers are seen as much more than simply cogs and wheels. What has changed in recent years is that the value knowledge workers in particular add comes not from the machines they operate but from the application of what they know.

As outdated as Taylorism may seem today, however, there is little doubt that it has had a profound effect on management this century, and was one of the first serious attempts to create a science of management. As the British champion of scientific management Lyndall Urwick noted in 1956:

> 'At the time Taylor began his work, business management as a discrete and identifiable activity had attracted little attention. It was usually regarded as incidental to, and flowing from knowledge-of/acquaintance-with a particular branch of manufacturing, the technical knowhow of making sausages or steel or shirts.'[4]

Taylor, then, helped put management on the map, and his work has had a profound impact throughout the world, leaving a lasting legacy that affects the way that managers make decisions even today. One might even go so far as to say that Taylor's emphasis on measurement foreshadowed the emergence of the total quality management (TQM) movement which still dominates many industries today.

In some ways, too, the concept of empowerment which has gained ground in recent years means that the role Taylor assigned to managers has been passed on to the people actually performing the tasks. They and not their bosses are now the ones who decide how the task can most effectively be performed.

UNIVERSAL PREDICTABILITY

This is the belief that everything is predictable. As naive as it sounds today, there was a time not so long ago when scientists thought that with sufficient computing power and enough data, they could predict anything.

The idea gained ground in the 1960s when the arrival of mainframe computers led to amazingly accurate calculations which paved the way for the US and Soviet space programmes.

The fact that scientists and engineers were able to accurately predict the force required to put a rocket in a given orbit and even to reach the Moon convinced some that all future events were knowable if the right information could be collected and the right laws of physics applied. In part, it was the incredible number-crunching power of the early computers which led them to this view.

In this way, some scientists began to believe that in time they could take the guesswork out of all decisions – making human decision-making obsolete. If all decisions were made by computers, they reasoned, there need never be another mistake.

By the 1980s, however, it dawned on the scientific community that some events simply could not be predicted. In particular, efforts to make long-range weather predictions were a dismal failure.

This gave rise to a new idea that any activity which involves nature or human beings is inherently unpredictable in the medium term. This paved the way for 'chaos theory'. But before dealing with chaos theory, another management model merits our attention.

TOTAL QUALITY MANAGEMENT (TQM)

It is not too much of a conceptual leap to suggest that universal predictability was a precursor to some of the ideas enshrined in the management approach known as total quality management (TQM).

In the past two decades TQM has become a by-word for efficiency and success throughout the business world. But its origins can be traced back to manufacturing companies in Japan in the period after the Second World War.

What these Japanese companies did was to analyze and document what was required of each worker to ensure a high-quality product. In this way they built consistency – or predictability – into their operating procedures so that every car or television set that rolled off the assembly line was of the same high standard, regardless of variable factors such as which workers were on that shift.

In this way, and in sharp contrast with other industrialized nations at the time, the Japanese were able to build-in quality to their management and manufacturing processes at a time when other companies fell well short of it. (Some readers may remember British Leyland in the 1970s, for example, when the term 'Friday car' was used to describe a substandard car that had apparently been built shoddily because workers were in a hurry to start their weekend.)

The philosophy of continuous improvement

So the Japanese companies had cracked the consistency problem. In addition, because the procedures in Japanese companies were documented, it was possible to continually make small improvements which enhanced the quality and productivity of work throughout the company.

It was largely due to the application of TQM among a highly disciplined workforce that Japanese companies were able to outperform their rivals in America and Europe during the 1970s to become the economic force they are today.

It is ironic, too, that two American management thinkers, Dr W Edwards Deming and Dr Joseph Juran, were instrumental in developing the approach that came to be known as TQM and which enabled the Japanese companies not only to catch up but to overtake leading US companies in the short space of 25 years.

For a while in the late 1970s and early 1980s, the Americans put the Japanese success story down to the availability of cheap labour. But when the Japanese car manufacturer Honda opened a plant in Marysville, Ohio, which used US workers paid at market rates and which outstripped the US car giants in Detroit, the penny finally dropped.[5]

American companies realized that the Japanese were doing something fundamentally different in their factories. The mid 1980s were characterized by a scramble among Western companies to understand how the Japanese companies were managed and to implement their own TQM initiatives. Indeed, such was the impact of TQM during this period that by the end of the 1980s it seemed possible almost to divide the world's top companies into two categories: those which had introduced TQM; and those which were just about to.

As with all good ideas, however, there was no clear consensus on the best way to apply TQM, and a great many variations on the theme emerged as different companies applied its basic tenets to their own circumstances.

Also, because it was applied first to heavy manufacturing processes, many of the TQM techniques that were developed at that time involved complex statistical analysis of variables such as temperature and material tolerances which are less easily applied to processes involving human interaction.

In reality, however, the success of TQM was in many respects less to do with the minutiae of these techniques and much more to do with the new patterns of thinking that it inspired.

It is in those terms that TQM has had the greatest impact on decision-making. At one level, of course, the decision to introduce TQM itself had a profound impact on the way organizations operated their manufacturing processes. But at another the philosophy of 'right first time' and 'zero

43

defects' which is at the heart of TQM has had a significant effect on the way that decisions are made in many organizations today.

So, too, has the reliance on empirical data and the drive to quantify inputs and measure the efficiency of processes. Out of the TQM movement as well has come a recognition that the participation of everyone in the organization is critical to success.

But let us return to chaos theory.

CHAOS THEORY

The popular understanding of chaos theory is that the universe is inherently chaotic and that the collision of seemingly unrelated events in one part of the universe can cause unpredicted consequences in another.

> 'Out of the TQM movement . . . has come a recognition that the participation of everyone in the organization is critical to success.'

This means that a small action can become magnified as it moves through a system, so that its eventual effect is much greater than the original action. So when someone says that a butterfly beating its wings in Britain could cause a tidal wave in China, it is a reference to the ideas contained in chaos theory.

(Jeff Goldblum you may recall played a chaotician in the film *Jurassic Park*. As such, he correctly predicted that there would be unforeseen consequences from meddling with nature by recreating dinosaurs from genetic material contained in traces of blood found in fossilized mosquitoes.)

Another example sometimes cited is that a cormorant diving into a lake in Central China could affect the weather in New York. As with the butterfly example, the idea is that a very small action can be magnified by a complex chain of events which eventually culminates in a much larger effect.

The ripples caused by the cormorant, for example, could – theoretically anyway – create a kind of domino effect, passing through nature as a wave or ripple of cause and effect which ultimately affects the weather in New York. So complex are these chains of events, chaos theory says that trying to understand them is futile.

However, scientists – chaoticians, anyway – draw an important distinction between three different states.

Stable equilibrium

This is a system where elements are in a state of balance, or if disturbed, will quickly return to a state of balance. As Neil Glass, a consultant with Gemini Consulting, points out in his book *Management Master-class*, for many years the washing powder market was a good example of a stable equilibrium. One company might improve its product and another launch a huge advertising campaign. But, in general, when the dust settled, market shares tended to settle into a position close to where they were before the change.[6]

Chaos (bounded instability)

A system where order and disorder co-exist. There are many unpredictable events but the basic patterns underlying the behaviour of elements can be analyzed and understood. Here, Glass offers the example of the car manufacturers. Sudden shocks such as a rise in oil prices and aggressive new competitors have caught some out, but the general trends have been detected and exploited by faster-moving firms.

Explosive instability

As the name suggests, this is a state where there is no order or pattern to a system. Events in a highly volatile system such as that created in the former Yugoslavia in the early 1990s illustrate this well.

Chaoticians might claim that many organizations that were formerly in something approaching stable equilibrium are now finding themselves in bounded instability or chaos. Denationalized airlines and banks are good examples, as are other organizations which find themselves in markets where rapid technological change can alter the competitive landscape almost overnight.

According to chaos theory, Glass observes, three key assumptions which underpinned decisions in the past no longer hold. These are as follows:

- **Assumption 1**: the organization is a simple 'closed system', so that what it decides to do will generally take place without too much disruption from outside.
- **Assumption 2**: the operating environment is sufficiently stable for management to understand it well enough to develop a detailed strategy.
- **Assumption 3**: there is sufficient understanding of the relationship between cause and effect for management to be able to pull on identifiable levers to bring about the changes it requires.

According to Glass, these old assumptions have been replaced by three new realities.

- **Reality 1**: organizations are complex 'open systems', deeply influenced by and influencing their environments. This means that actions may not have the results expected.

- **Reality 2**: the environment is changing so rapidly (continuously generating opportunities and threats) that top management cannot expect to formulate detailed strategies that are relevant by the time they are implemented.
- **Reality 3**: the simple linear models of cause and effect which traditional decision-making theory is based on have broken down. As a result, actions can have quite unexpected consequences.

Chaos theory is one good argument against universal predictability. It explains why we can never rely entirely on computers or any other completely rational system of analysis to make decisions for us.

Another body of thought or system of theory has also gained ground in the past 50 years, and has important implications for decision-making. It is known as 'game theory'.

GAME THEORY

John Von Neumann, the originator of game theory, is said to have based his ideas on watching the poker tables of the American Ivy League universities of Harvard and Princeton in the 1930s.

Von Neumann, a brilliant mathematician rather than a gambler, was concerned with human behaviour in game situations. His observations convinced him that no matter what the circumstances, there is always a strategy which will enable the game player to succeed. So, he argued, whether you are playing poker, negotiating pay deals or bidding in an auction, there are rules at work – albeit elusive rules – which if understood will enable the player to win.

Von Neumann himself went on to apply his talents to the development of US nuclear missiles and the first computer. But game theory attracted its own devotees who developed what management journalist and author Stuart Crainer has called 'its own Zen-like language of dilemmas and riddles'. The most famous of these is the 'prisoners' dilemma'.

The 'prisoners' dilemma'

Invented by Princeton's Albert Tucker in 1950, the 'prisoners' dilemma' is an imaginary scenario involving two prisoners accused of the same crime. During interrogation in separate cells they are each told that if one confesses and the other does not, the confessor will be released while the other will serve a long prison sentence. If neither confesses, both will be despatched to prison for a short sentence, and if both confess they will each receive an intermediate sentence.

By working through all the possibilities, the prisoners conclude that the best decision is to confess. As both reach the same decision they receive an intermediate sentence.

Game theory scenarios enjoyed a brief period of popularity in the 1950s and 1960s, but were seen mainly as intellectual exercises, rather than decision-making models. But interest in game theory was re-ignited in 1994 when the Nobel Prize for Economics was awarded to three distinguished game theorists – John Nash, John Harsanyi and Reinhard Selten. Each had built on the work of Von Neumann and Tucker to carry the discipline forward. Nash, for example, was the originator of 'Nash's equilibrium', an idea he developed in his PhD (which he completed at the tender age of 22).

The Nash equilibrium

This is the point at which no player can improve their position by changing strategy. Players in a game, Nash reasoned, will continue to change their strategy until this equilibrium position is reached. (In the 'prisoners' dilemma', for example, the 'Nash equilibrium' is reached when both prisoners acting on their own confess. At this point neither one can improve their position by changing strategy as this would risk a longer prison sentence.)

Game theory also suggests that a number of different types of game exist, with implications for the players.

Zero-sum game

A zero-sum game is one in which for every winner there is an equal and opposite loser. In other words, one player's gain is another player's loss. Most forms of gambling are necessarily zero-sum games. In roulette, for example, what the gambler loses the bank wins, and vice versa.

A good example of a zero-sum game in business is the competition for market share. But this is only a zero-sum game when the size of the market is static. If, on the other hand, new entrants increase the total market, then it can become a 'positive-sum game'.

Game theory has been influential in corporate decision-making over the past decade. However, the organizations which express an interest in it are usually from tightly regulated industries – such as power generation – or ones which operate in environments where there is limited competition or a cartel in operation.

Both situations tend to involve a limited number of players, playing by broadly accepted rules, and behaving in a rational manner. Under these circumstances, Game theory can provide a useful decision-making framework to understand what the best moves are.

(For the following examples I am indebted to an article by Stuart Crainer that appeared in *Management Today* in August 1996.)[7]

Cartels provide an especially rich source of examples. Take OPEC, the Organization of Petroleum Exporting Countries: the logic behind OPEC is that oil producers club together to fix the price of crude oil. This relies on the participating members agreeing on how much oil they will produce – thus creating what game theorists call an 'equilibrium'. All cartel members benefit from a price that maximizes long-term profits.

In reality, however, all it takes is for one rogue member to ignore its quotas in search of short-term gain and the equilibrium is destabilized. The 'greedy country' makes higher profits temporarily, but the price falls and other members of the cartel soon follow suit. In the 1980s, for example, chaos reigned and the price of a barrel of crude oil fell from US$30 to US$10.

In other cases, companies are merely delaying the inevitable results of the game. Rather than blatantly disregarding its rules, they create diversionary tactics to postpone the inevitable checkmate. This is the corporate version of the schoolboys' game of 'chicken'.

The battle between the Channel tunnel and the cross-Channel ferry companies is a case in point. In the end, as Crainer points out, there can only be one winner of this particular game – the tunnel. Logic suggests that the ferry companies should keep their prices up as they would lose any price war – and game theorists predict that at some point in the future this is precisely what will happen. In the interim, however, the ferry companies are playing a game of chicken.

They know that, whatever they do, the tunnel will remain. A ferry can be decommissioned; a large and expensive tunnel cannot. On the other hand, saddled with enormous debts Eurotunnel could go bust, so the ferry companies try to push Eurotunnel's management as far as possible without precipitating an all-out price war. It is a game of brinkmanship with Eurotunnel being tempted to join a price war it would ultimately win, but can ill afford.

There are many other examples. In the UK, for example, in recent years there have been the petrol price wars among the supermarkets and the oil companies, and the newspaper price wars. Each of these has echoes of game theory.

As Crainer points out:

'The key lesson from this and other scenarios explored by game theory is simply that the interactions of companies and other orga-

nizations are interdependent. What you do interacts or impacts on the possible choices of others in your situation or industry. Success depends not only on what you do, brilliantly calculated though it may be, but on how others respond and act.

'In fact, despite being rational to the nth degree, game theory encompasses some of the fundamental truths of decision-making. If a company decides to make an investment it should consider how others – whether they be competitors, customers or suppliers – will react. Game theory acknowledges that real life is not conducted in a vacuum where A + B inevitably produces C.'

Allocentrism

In game theory terminology, 'allocentrism' means putting yourself in the other guy's shoes to consider his future moves and their likely impact. A topical example is the decision about Britain's involvement in the European Union, in particular whether it should opt to be part of a European single currency.

Most of the rhetoric surrounding this issue to date has regarded the actions of the UK in isolation – whereas in reality the dynamics are much more complex. If, for example, Britain chooses to go its own way, that decision is likely to precipitate a chain of events and actions, not only by other member states but by other countries outside, including America and Japan.

The same principles apply to companies. Comments David Stout of London Business School:

'Perfect certainty does not exist. Everything is interdependent and every company's development is a fruition of major moves by it and other companies.'

Stout attributes the increasing interest in game theory to

'economists coming to terms with the fact that they are dealing with real people. Decisions are made on imprecise information and beliefs in the likely behaviour of other contenders'.

Just how helpful game theory is for decision-makers, of course, depends on your point of view. As Stefan Szymanski, senior lecturer in economics at Imperial College Management School, explains:

'Game theory is about making predictions about behaviour if people follow their own best interests. It doesn't provide a solution. Rather, it is a way of thinking about the future; a tool to get people to think.'

Stimulating as it may be, the 'prisoners' dilemma', too, has a fundamental flaw. As Dr Eddie Obeng, founder of Pentacle, the Virtual Business School, points out:

> **'Just how helpful game theory is for decision-makers, of course, depends on your point of view.'**

> *'Decision-making and risk-taking are individualistic; human arts rather than mathematical sciences. The prisoners are prone to human frailty and emotions. Most real-life business situations are not zero-sum games. If you lose market share, it does not necessarily follow that your competitors gain market share. The outcomes aren't fixed, predictable or calculable. Game theory is great for the textbooks but very difficult to apply to real life.'*

Win-win situations

What game theory can do is help decision-makers reconsider strategies driven by win–lose scenarios and begin to explore the merits of alternative strategies that could yield win–win situations with mutual benefits for themselves, their customers and even their competitors.

The notion of a set of rules which apply to any given situation underpins much of the management theory developed in the past 30 years. (Indeed, it could be argued that it has been the driving force behind economic theory since its infancy.)

The application of such ideas has created a set of models and tools to explain the competitive position of companies in the marketplace. We will consider some of these in the next chapter.

References

1. March, J, and Cyert, R, *A Behavioural Theory of the Firm*, New York, 1963.

2. Taylor, F W, *The Principles of Scientific Management*, Harper & Row, New York, 1911.

3. Crainer, S, *Key Management Ideas*, Pitman, 1996.

4. Urwick, L (editor), *The Golden Book of Management*, Newman Neame, London, 1956.

5. Clutterbuck, David, and Dearlove, Des, 'The Charity as a Business', *Directory of Social Change*, 1996.

6. Glass, Neil, *Management Masterclass*, Nicholas Brealey, 1996.

7. Crainer, Stuart, *Management Today*, August 1996.

3

The decision-makers' tool-box

'Theorists teach how to construct decision trees; and
how to marry the trees with probability theory, so
that the degree of risk along each branch and twig
can be metered. But no manager uses the trees, the
branches or the twigs.'
ROBERT HELLER, business journalist

As is the case with so many other areas of management, a whole host of tools and techniques have been invented over the years to help managers make better decisions. Some of these tools are very simple, some are more complex. How helpful any tool is, of course, depends on who is using it and for what purpose.

As the quote at the beginning of the chapter suggests, however, it is questionable whether managers really use such tools to make real decisions. But a knowledge of them allows readers to make up their own minds (in any case, no book on decision-making would be complete without an account of at least some of the techniques available). It is for this reason that we venture once more into the realms of theory.

> **'How helpful any tool is . . . depends on who is using it and for what purpose.'**

Also included are summaries of a number of techniques and models which have been created to help strategic decision-makers. Here we consider:

- decision trees
- fishbone diagrams
- flow charts
- brown papering (process mapping)
- mind maps

prioritizing tools such as:

- the ABC method
- workset (colour coding)
- Delphi technique

analysis tools, including:

- SWOT analysis
- Porter's five competitive forces
- the Boston matrix
- the directional policy matrix
- other matrices, such as the Ansoff matrix

- cost-benefit analysis (CBA)
- ABC analysis (activity-based costing)
- ABM (activity-based management)

others:

- scenario planning
- flipping a coin.

DECISION TREES

The decision tree is probably the best known of all decision-making tools. A decision tree is essentially a graphic representation of the options flowing from an initial decision. So, to use an often quoted example, a decision tree might be drawn up for a decision to build a new factory.

The decision tree (see Figure 3.1) sets out alternative courses of action and the financial implications of each alternative. By assigning probabilities to the likelihood of events, the decision tree can be used to understand the implications of a decision or set of decisions.

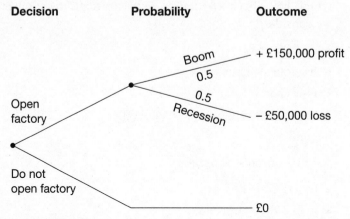

Figure 3.1 Decision tree

FISHBONE DIAGRAMS (THE ISHIKAWA METHOD)

Fishbone diagrams (named for their appearance) were originally invented by Professor Kaoru Ishikawa of the University of Tokyo, which explains why their use is sometimes referred to as the 'Ishikawa method'.

The fishbone diagram is a diagnostic tool. It helps the user to understand the relationship between cause and effect and is especially useful in situations where the causes of a problem or crisis cannot be easily

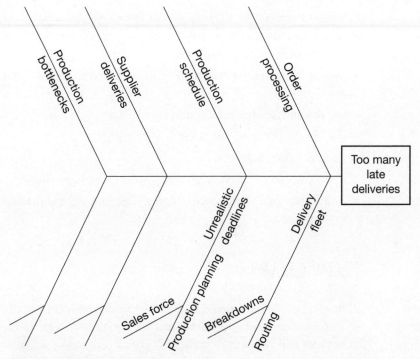

Figure 3.2 Fishbone diagram

measured. In such situations, a fishbone diagram can help clarify the major issues involved in a decision. A simple example (see Figure 3.2) serves to illustrate how this tool works.

The steps involved are as follows.

1. State the problem in a box on the right-hand side of a blank sheet of paper (the head of the fish).
2. Draw a horizontal line coming out from the box (the fish's spine).
3. Ask the question 'What is causing the problem?', and write each possible reason on a line at 45 degrees to the horizontal line (to make the fish's ribs).
4. Ask what might lie behind each of the possible reasons making up the ribs and add each new reason as smaller bones coming off the ribs.
5. Assess the linkages between the main reasons and sub-reasons to understand how they might be connected or whether they are duplicated elsewhere on the diagram.

The resulting diagram should enable the decision-maker to have a much better overview of the factors that might be causing the problem. As Alan Barker notes,[1] fishbone diagrams allow the manager to:

- focus on the overall problem rather than simply parts
- find more than one possible cause – countering the illusion of a simple cause–effect relationship
- escape from 'squirrel-caging' – obsessive attention to a tiny part of a problem
- see the linkages between causes more clearly
- discuss the problem in a team or with a group
- generate new ideas
- counter possessiveness of ideas in group decision-making
- establish a logical sequence of actions for tackling the problem: plans, priorities, etc.

FLOW CHARTS

A flow chart, or flow diagram, is a pictorial representation of the flow of information, ideas, or components through a system. In business, a flow chart will typically be used to illustrate a process – whether it is the physical process in a production line or the management process by which tasks are completed.

For example, a flow chart would be one way to explain the steps involved in producing a widget, or even the way that decisions are made within the organization. Each stage in the process is represented by a box and the boxes are connected up, with arrows showing the direction – or flow – through the system. Where the next step is depends on the previous outcome, which can also be indicated (typically with a 'yes' or 'no' branch).

Flow charts are an excellent way to explain or understand what is happening within a closed system. In particular, they can be used as a diagnostic tool to aid decision-making, providing a better understanding of where the problem might lie, or identifying possible actions or alternatives.

For the sake of easy recognition, the convention when drawing flow diagrams is to represent:

- statements of fact in oval boxes
- questions in diamond boxes
- actions in rectangular boxes
- direction of flow as arrows.

Figures 7.1 and 7.2 in Chapter 7 show flow diagrams to depict two different approaches to managing mistakes – the 'sweep-it-under-the-carpet school of management' and the learning organization. (See pages 153 and 154.)

Try drawing a flow diagram for the decision-making process in your organization. Or, if you're feeling brave, for the way it manages mistakes. Now use the diagram to identify where improvements could be made.

Using the flow chart, a number of issues can be considered, such as:

- Are there any steps in the process which can be eliminated to reduce costs or save time?
- Is there a more efficient way to organize the flow?
- Does the whole process require re-engineering because it is out of date?
- Should it be scrapped altogether?

BROWN PAPERING (PROCESS MAPPING)

Another technique which can be used to understand a process is brown papering. This tool is described by Neil Glass, a management consultant with Gemini Consulting, in his book *Management Masterclass*.[2]

Brown papering is useful for tracing what really happens in a process. When managers try to explain the process flows in the organization, because they don't actually carry out the tasks, they often end up showing how work should be done rather than what actually happens. As a result, they often miss the root cause of a problem or key areas where improvements could be made.

Brown papering is a way to ensure that the flow is accurately portrayed. Typically, it involves interviewing the people who carry out the work at each stage to understand the main activities, information flows, and connections. A rough idea of the process can then be drawn on a sheet of paper.

The next stage is to pin up a long sheet of brown paper – usually between four and six metres long – and map out the process using Post-it notes, sheets of paper and key documents. The people originally interviewed are then invited to review their part of the process to ensure that what has been constructed is an accurate description.

Once this stage has been completed, the people involved in the process or affected by it are invited to 'walk through the brown paper model', adding suggestions for improvements on Post-it notes as they go. Once this has been done, the comments form the basis of the next stage: re-drawing the brown paper process diagram to eliminate problems.

The beauty of this technique is that improvements can be tested by asking people to walk the new process, before any expensive final decisions are made.

MIND MAPS

Mind mapping is a way to simultaneously represent many different strands of a complex issue. Invented by the psychologist and author Tony Buzan, it can be used to generate ideas, or memorize complex systems or concepts. It also provides an excellent tool for communicating complicated ideas to others.

The basic principle is simple. The manager takes the central idea, problem or issue, and writes it down in the middle of a large sheet of paper. Ideas triggered by the main theme are then represented as a series of lines coming out from the centre, with subsidiary ideas or issues coming off these, so that the overall appearance of the mind map is similar to a spider's web, or the root system of a tree, with lines spreading out towards the edge of the paper in all directions.

Mind mapping makes it possible to break down conventional, linear ways of thinking about problems. By representing ideas in a messy, seemingly haphazard way, it frees people from the need to order their thoughts or to impose prior logic. This allows them to approach problems quite literally with a blank sheet of paper.

In fact, the strength of this tool is that it is completely unstructured. The user can go off in any direction and make any link or jump that comes to mind. In many ways, mind mapping is the pictorial equivalent of brainstorming, where a group of people take an issue and throw out any thoughts or ideas that pop into their brains.

With both brainstorming and mind mapping, if it isn't messy, then you aren't doing it right.

PRIORITIZING TOOLS

There are lots of tools and techniques for helping managers prioritize their work and decisions, including:

- the ABC method
- workset (colour coding).

The ABC method

A simple, but effective, way of prioritizing tasks and decisions is to allocate them as A, B or C tasks according to their importance. (It's a technique that can also be used for editing speeches and reports that are too long. In this case, points designated C are the ones which can most sensibly be discarded.)

- A tasks are the top priority.
- B tasks are those which, while still important are less of a priority, but which might become next week's priorities.
- C tasks are those which while deserving attention sooner or later can be put on a back burner.
- D tasks are tasks that don't need to be done at all and should be dumped.

Where there is a time factor involved (as there often is), tasks can also be given an A, B or C classification for urgency. So an important decision that is also urgent would be denoted AA (double A).

In this way, managers can quickly determine the order in which they should tackle tasks. It also allows them to identify important decisions which might otherwise get put off because of more urgent but unimportant tasks.

Workset (colour coding)

By the same token, some managers use coloured dots to prioritize tasks. Management writer Meredith Belbin has even conducted experiments using a colour coding system to help managers prioritize and clarify the work of the people who report to them.

He calls the technique 'workset', and it involves the use of four core colours for managing tasks. These are used to classify the work of subordinates into 'tasks' and 'responsibilities', and denote whether these are personal or shared

So, for example, *blue work* refers to tasks that a job-holder has to carry out in a prescribed way to an approved standard; whereas *yellow* signifies work where an individual has responsibility for meeting objectives in any way he or she sees fit.

Employees then monitor the time they spend on different coloured tasks and feed back the results to managers. They can also use three extra colours to signify time not covered by the core colours – for example, *pink* for work which demands their presence, but leads to no useful results.

When the system was piloted recently among staff at the Royal Leicester Infirmary, the results were encouraging, with staff reporting that it facilitated a more meaningful discussion of work with managers, improved teamwork and reduced the number of words used in job specifications by 90 per cent. This sort of system will no doubt appeal to some people more than others.

Delphi technique

This is a forecasting technique using a number of experts (or managers) who each make estimates in round one, then receive everyone else's estimates and re-estimate in round two, and so on until consensus is reached. It has its uses.

ANALYSIS TOOLS

Much beloved of management consultants, business analysis of one kind or another underpins much of what can be called scientific management. In the last 50 years, numerous tools have been developed to help managers analyze situations and make rational decisions.

There is no way of knowing which of these tools is useful and which are merely elegant techniques for justifying the fees charged by management consultants. On the whole, however, it is reasonable to assume that taken all together – with a large pinch of salt – these tools have made a positive net contribution to the effectiveness of decision-making within organizations.

The tools below are some of the simpler ones, but also some of the most useful.

SWOT analysis

Perhaps the best-known – and most basic – of all analytical tools is SWOT analysis. This involves a review of strengths/weaknesses/opportunities/threats.

In the main, strengths and weaknesses will pertain to the organization itself; while opportunities and threats are more likely to arise from features of the external environment. So, a SWOT analysis might be used when deciding whether to enter a new market in Eastern Europe.

- **Strengths:** what the organization is good at, particularly areas in which it has an advantage over other organizations. For example, a strong brand name, or low operating costs.
- **Weaknesses:** areas where the organization is at a disadvantage compared to the competition. For example, low levels of specialist knowledge about the new market, or poor geographical coverage in the region.
- **Opportunities:** trends or circumstances that favour the organization or provide an opening which it can fill. For example, contacts in the

region that present opportunities to form strategic partnerships, or growing demand for its products.

- **Threats:** developments that are potentially dangerous. For example, a competitor building a new factory in the region, or political instability.

From the SWOT analysis, a clearer picture of the likely outcome of the decision should emerge.

Porter's five competitive forces

Michael Porter, an American management academic, is regarded as one of the most influential business thinkers of his generation. In his 1980 book *Competitive Strategy: Techniques for Analyzing Industries and Competitors* he set out a model still regarded by many as essential reading for strategic decision-makers.[3]

'In any industry, whether it is domestic or international or produces a product or a service, the rules of competition are embodied in five competitive forces', he wrote.

Porter's five competitive forces are the following.

1. **The entry of new competitors:** new competition necessitates some sort of competitive response which will inevitably require resources, thus reducing profits.

2. **The threat of substitutes:** the presence of viable alternatives to your product or service in the marketplace, will mean that the prices you can charge will be limited.

3. **The bargaining power of buyers:** if customers have bargaining power, they will use it. This will reduce profit margins and, as a result, affect profitability.

4. **The bargaining power of suppliers:** given power over you, suppliers will increase their prices and adversely affect your profitability.

5. **Rivalry among existing competitors:** competition leads to the need to invest in marketing, R&D or price reductions, which will reduce your profits.

These five forces provide a way for companies to understand the competitive markets in which they operate. They can be interpreted as the 'rules of the game', which have to be acted on and challenged if a company is to change its competitive position within its marketplace. In other words, they are the levers upon which any strategy must act on if it is to be successful.

The Boston matrix

The Boston matrix is a tool for analyzing the strategic position of a particular business within a portfolio. During the 1970s, a number of these sorts of tools were developed to help companies classify their component businesses. Of these, the matrix developed by the Boston Consulting Group (BCG) is probably the best-known.

During the 1960s, it was fashionable for companies to diversify into new business areas to offset the effects of a downturn in existing markets and also to provide new investment alternatives for mature industries. This led to the growth of large, centrally controlled companies with fingers in many pies. But a number of shocks to the world economy, including the oil crises of the early 1970s, persuaded companies that highly centralized planning was dangerous. At that time companies began to realize that their centres no longer 'knew best'.

This led to a new approach, where conglomerates – made up of portfolios of businesses – allowed greater autonomy to managers running the business. Under the new model, the centre was seen more as a 'banker' deciding where to invest its money to maximize the return. As such, it needed some way to categorize the businesses in its portfolio. The Boston matrix (or box) was one of the tools they looked to for help

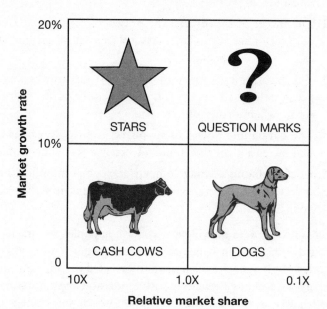

Figure 3.3 The Boston matrix

as it provided a simple framework for clarifying investment decisions according to the future potential of the individual businesses.

The Boston matrix, sometimes called the 'Dog/star' matrix for obvious reasons, actually started life in the 1960s as the growth/share matrix. Still much quoted, this analysis tool epitomized a sort of generic view of strategic decision-making.

It is, in fact, a simple two-by-two matrix (a format popular with management consultants ever since) which measures market growth and relative market share for all the businesses in the company's portfolio. Each business can be placed on the matrix and classified accordingly.

- **Stars** are businesses with high growth rates and low market share. They represent excellent investment opportunities.
- **Cash cows** have low growth and low market share, making them cash generators, to be defended with investment if required.
- **Question marks** have high growth and high market share and should be watched carefully to see where they are moving.
- **Dogs** have the worst combination – high market share and low growth – and are best disposed of.

The Boston matrix envisages that its analysis applies across all markets. In other words, rather than seeing a dynamic set of forces that are unique to any given marketplace, it asserts that once the current position is properly understood, then the effect of an investment decision is predictable. The skill lies then in accurately understanding where the business is in the first place. The options flow from that, and the outcome of decisions, in a sense, are pre-determined.

The idea was that the company's centre would analyze its portfolio of businesses using the matrix and base its decision on the following.

- **Stars:** build.
- **Cash cows:** harvest.
- **Question marks:** hold and monitor.
- **Dogs:** withdraw.

The directional policy matrix

Other conceptual frameworks followed. Royal Dutch/Shell, for example, took BCG's original matrix a stage further with its directional policy matrix.

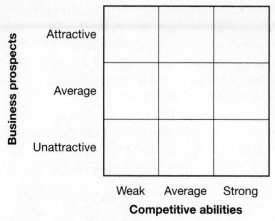

Figure 3.4 The directional policy matrix

Other matrices

In recent years, too, BCG has championed other frameworks. But BCG does not have a monopoly. There is also 'Roger's box', which offers a hypothesis on how executives should spend their time; the Ansoff matrix, named after Igor Ansoff (see Figure 3.5), and Blake and Mouton's 'managerial grid' which measures managers against two dimensions – their concern for people and concern for completing tasks. The list is endless. No self-respecting business journal article would be complete without a conceptual map or framework.

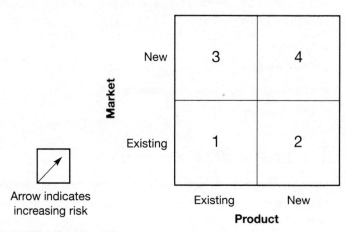

Figure 3.5 The Ansoff matrix

Cost-benefit analysis (CBA)

CBA is a monetary assessment of a project's worth which compares all its costs and benefits. It is often used to assess public-sector projects where an attempt is made to quantify social benefits; it can also be used by private-sector managers to take account of *soft* benefits of a

'No self-respecting business journal article would be complete without a conceptual map or framework.'

major project. In CBA all the benefits and costs of a project or decision are listed and quantified.

CBA is less popular with the private sector, but is finding new favour with some executives. It can be used to evaluate projects that are thought to have major but indirect value, such as a corporate identity programme. Even approximate quantification of soft benefits can be useful, provided CBA is not used to justify decisions already taken.

ABC analysis (activity-based costing)

This is a recent and important method of ensuring that all costs, and especially indirect costs and overheads, are properly allocated to particular products. Traditional costing methods allocated indirect costs via cost centres, which was an imprecise method.[4]

This did not matter so much when direct costs were the majority of the cost structure, but today many products comprise a greater amount of indirect than direct cost. Using the old methods tended to under-allocate cost to special products and services using a lot of indirect cost, resulting in average costing and average pricing, i.e., pricing standard products too high and specials too low. ABC avoids this by allocating indirect costs better by identifying the cost drivers for each activity. At least, that's what the experts say.

ABC works as follows.

1. The activities and objects (usually products, but sometimes customers or other relevant definitions) are defined. This can be a time-consuming process. For example, if a customer demands being supplied with two products, or special terms, it is more relevant to look at customer than individual product profitability.

2. The cost drivers (what determines cost – for example, the number of work orders) are defined in relation to each activity.

3. The costs are then allocated to each object and compared to price to determine profitability.

ABC can also be turned into an accounting system, but it is really a way of analyzing product profitability at a point in time. As the cost drivers and activities can change, ABC analysis needs to be revisited periodically to ensure that the previous data and insights are still valid. ABC should lead to changed decisions about pricing, product and customer focus, market share policy and other actions that can raise profitability.

ABM (activity-based management)

This is an extension of ABC (activity-based costing) which makes it a whole philosophy of management by taking customers' needs into consideration and working out where the extra cost of special products or services can be fully or more than fully recovered from customers. ABM has not yet achieved anything like the popularity of ABC, but it is a logical outgrowth of it and the focus on customer utility can be useful.

This ends our brief look at analysis – apart from a discussion of paralysis of analysis in Chapter 5. (There are plenty of books on the subject for those who want to know more.) But the remainder of this chapter is better devoted to another technique, or tool; one which presents an exciting new challenge to decision-makers everywhere.

SCENARIO PLANNING

Scenario planning may prove to be one of the most important decision-making tools in the manager's tool-box. For this reason, and because it is widely misunderstood, this technique merits a lengthier discussion.

Although only now coming into wider use, scenario planning has been practised in one form or another in the business world since the early 1960s. It was first used by a far-sighted team of planners at the oil company Royal Dutch Shell. Using the technique, they foresaw the energy crises of 1973 and 1979, the growth of energy conservation, the evolution of the global environmental movement, and even the break-up of the Soviet Union, years before these events happened.

But it took the publication of two recent books, one by a former Shell manager Arie de Geus and the other by Art Kleiner, who interviewed Shell managers – to put scenario planning firmly on the management agenda.

Timely as it is, however, some believe that even Shell has been guilty of taking its eye off the ball recently in allowing environmental pressure groups to dictate the pace of change. Other companies have much to learn if the technique is to yield results.

As de Geus notes in his book *The Living Company*,[5] today scenario planning *'remains surrounded by vagueness and an air of mystery. People are unsure whether it is a process for reaching better decisions; a way to know the future better; or a combination of both.'*

In fact, say many of those who use the technique, it is a way to facilitate lateral thinking in an organization. Although sometimes confused with disaster planning or contingency planning – which deals with how a company should respond when things go wrong – scenario planning is a way to identify both threats and opportunities that flow from decisions.

'Thinking the unthinkable': origins of scenario planning

The technique was invented by Herman Kahn, the famous futurist from the Rand Corporation and the Hudson Institute. But the term 'scenario' – meaning a detailed outline for the plot of a future film – was borrowed from Hollywood by Kahn's friend, screenwriter and novelist Leo Rosten.

'These stories about the future were aimed at helping people break past their mental blocks and consider the "unthinkable" futures, which would take them by surprise if they weren't prepared', explains Art Kleiner in *The Age of Heretics*.[6] 'The point was not to make accurate predictions (although like all futurists he [Kahn] gleefully loved being right), but to come up with a mythic story that brings the point home.'

Kahn himself was best known for his scenarios about nuclear war – and his trademark phrase 'thinking the unthinkable'. Other early pioneers of scenario thinking also tended to look at the macro-level – the future of mankind, for example, or the economy of an entire region. This seemed to place the technique firmly in the domain of senior management strategists.

SCENARIO PLANNING IN SHELL

What Shell realized was that managers need a translation of these grand scenarios into something more recognizable. The plot needs to be focused on a particular audience or issue. In fact, learning to focus scenarios on a specific business purpose was part of the company's contribution to the practice.

In the 1970s, planners at Shell began to build on Kahn's work, developing their own version of the scenario approach as a possible answer to two questions: 'how do we look up to 20 to 30 years' ahead?' and 'how can we get people to discuss the "unthinkable" together?'

It is no coincidence, of course, that the technique is coming to the fore now at a time when so many seemingly unassailable companies have been wrongfooted by changes in their trading environments. If only IBM had seen that the PC offered an alternative future to mainframe computers, for example, its position today would be very different.

Wind tunnelling

So, how does scenario planning work? Scenarists talk about 'wind tunnelling' strategies and policies. In effect, each scenario – or story about the future – represents a different set of conditions in the wind tunnel. A policy or strategy decision is the prototype aircraft which must be tested in the wind tunnel to see how it performs under varying conditions. A decision may stand up well in one scenario, the argument goes, but the wings could drop off in another.

Professor Kees van der Heijden at Strathclyde University is a leading authority on the subject. As head of scenario planning at Shell in the 1980s, his team was responsible for developing scenarios that, among other things, looked at the impact of environmental issues on Shell's business.

> 'Traditional planning is based on identifying trends and extrapolating into the future. But no matter how good the analysis, it is always a projection of the past. Yet we know the future is uncertain, and that there is more than one possible future that a company may have to operate in.
>
> 'As with traditional planning, the starting point with scenario planning is to try to identify what is predictable and what is not. But the scenario planner tries to get behind the trends or patterns to understand the "driving forces". These make up the "causal texture" or mental model which gives a common structure for scenarios. It is possible then to develop a number of stories within that structure representing different conditions or futures.'[7]

As Tony Hodgson, managing director of the Idon Group, a consultancy specializing in scenario planning, notes, this is a radical departure for most companies.

> 'One thing we're not very good at is entertaining several equally plausible futures. What organizations in particular tend to do is take a bet on one future and plan accordingly.
>
> 'But once you accept that you can't predict the future, then you can consider alternative scenarios. You start to see the need for what we call "multi-future thinking" – entertaining several very

different but equally plausible futures. What you have to avoid is falling into the trap of trying to see which one is the most likely.'

Learning to live with ambiguity

'Scenario planning is about living with ambiguity', says Hodgson. 'If managers can look at their own issues and ambiguities and come up with scenarios which can be used to test ideas and decisions, then that is a very powerful tool.'

Professor van der Heijden agrees: 'Operational decisions should be wind-tunnelled in the same way as top-level strategy. It could relate to recruitment, reward levels, or skills training, but what you try to do is see how a decision will perform under different scenarios.'

According to Professor van der Heijden, however, an important aspect of scenario planning is the recognition that despite the uncertainty, there is an element of predictability about the future.

'Scenarists like to emphasize uncertainty and ambiguity because it is in that area that their approach is different. But if you cannot predict anything about the future then even thinking about it would be futile. Fortunately there is predictability around us as well as uncertainty. Scenarios should be as much about prediction as uncertainty.

'If we look at a new situation everything may look terribly ambiguous. The art is to find out how much of this ambiguity is due to ignorance and limited perspective and how much due to inherent uncertainty. Scenario planning can help us do that. But it requires a lot of hard work. It is not a free lunch.'

At Shell, he says, scenarios are used at all levels. Every project – whether it's a decision to build this refinery or go into that oil field – has to be wind-tunnelled first.

'It's a rule of the game if you want to get senior management buy-in. There is a whole cultural dimension to scenarios that is very liberating. It leads to a much more open-minded approach.'

Flying with the radar on

According to Clem Sunter, head of scenario planning at Anglo American Corporation and another leading authority on the technique:

'Scenarios are to organizations what radar is to a pilot. They help us look for the first signs of changes that can profoundly affect how we work, and make us think about our responses.'

CASE STUDY: SOUTH AFRICA

One of the most powerful demonstrations of how scenario planning can make a difference was in South Africa, where it was instrumental in changing the mind-set of the people.

In the mid 1980s, Clem Sunter, head of scenario planning at Anglo American Corporation was asked by the De Klerk government to put together some scenarios for what would happen following Nelson Mandela's release. Sunter visited Mandela in prison and talked to key members of De Klerk's cabinet.

Based on those discussions, Sunter and other members of his team gave numerous lectures to the public outlining scenarios for South Africa to the year 2000. The country, they said, could all too easily revert to civil war, with tragic consequences. But at the same time they challenged South Africans to 'think the unthinkable'. What if all South Africans sat down at a negotiating table to work out a new constitution peacefully instead of having a civil war? What if sanctions were lifted and trade resumed with the rest of the world?

As Sunter himself notes:

'By presenting a positive future for South Africa as a possibility when all around were so utterly negative about the country's prospects, we helped change the direction of the national debate.'

Scenario writing

- When writing scenarios avoid 'good news' and 'bad news' scenarios. They should be subtly different rather than extremes. Each scenario should be a different story of the future with a different plot.

- There must be more than one scenario. Some schools of thought say two is best; any more than four or five and it becomes too complicated.

- Each scenario should be a detailed 'story' of a possible future. The detail depends on the importance of the project.

- The aim is not to predict the future, but to provide alternatives which can be used to 'wind-tunnel' strategies or plans.

FLIPPING A COIN

Finally, in this chapter, let us consider one of the oldest and perhaps most under-rated decision-making techniques: flipping a coin. From the sublime to the ridiculous, you may think, but, used sensibly, there's more to this technique than meets the eye.

First and foremost, it's important to recognize that a tool is only as good as the purpose for which it is used. A surgeon would no more use a hammer to perform intricate heart surgery than you would a scalpel – or laser – to bang in a nail.

Flipping a coin is only effective as a tool when a decision involves choosing between competing alternatives. It has absolutely no diagnostic or analytical properties whatsoever. At least, it has no analytical properties that most management consultants would admit to.

In fact, in the hands of an accomplished decision-maker, a coin can be a much more subtle instrument than any of the other tools discussed in this chapter. Flipping a coin can tell you what your conscious mind cannot – what your intuition is trying to say.

Heads I win, tails I win, too

Given that there is a 50:50 chance of getting heads or tails, only a fool, a gambler (or a desperate manager) would put their faith in the outcome of flipping a coin. But faced with a situation where you are unable to decide between two options, it is surprising how effective the technique can be.

Say, for example, you are trying to decide between accepting a new job or remaining in your current job. There are pluses and minuses on both sides: the new job means a higher salary,

> '. . . a tool is only as good as the purpose for which it is used.'

better company car, and more challenge. But it also means moving house or commuting an extra 100 miles a day. If you take the new position you could also be out of work within 12 months if the project you're taking on doesn't get senior management buy-in. Better the Devil you know, then?

But your current company is also laying off managers in your department and despite assurances from your boss, who knows when your number might come up – or his for that matter? Let us assume, too, that your partner doesn't want to move, and the kids really like the school they're at.

On the other hand, the extra money from the new job would be useful and the experience would greatly enhance your CV. What do you do?

The chances are, you end up 'squirrel-caging' – an exhausting condition where both sides of the argument race around in your brain like an excited squirrel in a cage. No sooner do you decide to take the new job than you think of another reason to stay put. And on it goes.

This is the moment to trust your intuition, but how do you quieten all those other voices so you can hear what it's saying? Cometh the hour, cometh the tool – in this case the trusty coin.

Listening to the voice of intuition

To do this properly, you need to gather your family – or others with vested interests – together in one room, but they have to remain silent while the ceremony of the coin takes place. If possible, get one of them to perform the honours.

Now you're ready. Clear your mind of everything but the coin. Heads you take the new job, tails you stay put. And go!

The coin is flipped into the air, spinning over and over, and is plucked out of the air and slapped onto a wrist. It's heads. That means you take the job – how do you feel at this instant? Pleased? Relieved? Or disappointed? Miserable? Daunted?

The voice you hear is your intuition. Listen to it and make your decision accordingly.

References

1. Barker, Alan, *How to be a Better Decision-maker*, Kogan Page, 1996.

2. Glass, Neil, *Management Masterclass*, Nicholas Brealey, 1996.

3. Porter, M., *Competitive Strategy: Techniques for Analyzing Industries and Competitors*, Free Press, New York, 1980.

4. Crainer, Stuart, *The FT Management Handbook*, Pitman, 1996.

5. de Geus, Arie, *The Living Company*, Nicholas Brealey, 1997.

6. Kleiner, Art, *The Age of Heretics*, Nicholas Brealey, 1996.

7. Author interview.

The hare and the tortoise

'Work expands to fill the time available for its completion.'
C Northcote Parkinson, *Parkinson's Law*

So do decisions.

'I am a tortoise, and M&S is a tortoise. We don't do things unless we have thought them through very carefully.'
Sir Richard Greenbury,
chairman of Marks & Spencer

'The broad-ranging strategic plan is no longer a guarantee of success. The premium now is on moving fast and keeping pace.'
Professor Kathleen Eisenhardt,
Stanford Business School

Timing is said to be the golden rule of comedy. Every one of us at some time or another has suffered at the hands of bad timing when a joke that was hilarious when someone else told it falls flat when repeated. By the same token, we have all laughed at an old joke we've heard many times when it is delivered by a true comedian.

The secret of effective decision-making, too, is timing. Some decisions – those arising from immediate opportunities or threats – have to be taken very quickly with the information available. There are others, however, where an immediate decision is not required and it pays to leave the options open: whether Britain should join a single European currency, perhaps. As indicated earlier, some decisions may not need to be made at all.

In this chapter we look at:

- hares and tortoises – the different ways managers approach decisions
- fast impressions
- pigeon-holing decisions
- evaluating time-scales
- time management
- the 80/20 principle
- crisis management
- the nimble organization
- just-in-time decisions.

> 'The secret of effective decision-making . . . is timing.'

THE DIFFERENT WAYS MANAGERS APPROACH DECISIONS

In business, as in life, some decision-makers are hares and some are tortoises. When presented with a set of circumstances, some people reach conclusions very quickly, while others prefer to mull over the facts for a long time before making a pronouncement. Both types of managers have their uses, but recognizing which of the two you tend towards can help you become a more effective decision-maker.

Whichever you are, there is some good news and some bad news.

Hares

Hares, for example, can:

- assimilate ideas and information very rapidly to form a picture of what is happening
- see short cuts that others miss
- make decisions based on whatever facts are available
- react quickly to opportunities and threats
- make decisions at the drop of a hat
- spot a change of paradigm and seize the opportunity it presents
- wing it, if necessary.

But hares also tend to:

- look for short cuts when it would be better to go the long way round
- be intolerant of details
- miss things in their hurry to move on to the next task
- rely on superficial explanations for complex problems
- be impatient of others who slow things down, especially tortoises, who they see as plodders
- wing it when it's not necessary
- have a limited attention span
- see only one side of the story
- make rash decisions when it would be better to wait and see.

Tortoises

Tortoises, on the other hand, can:

- assimilate complex and detailed information to form a rounded view
- see both sides of the story
- be very patient when things take longer than expected
- stay with something until it is finished
- be methodical
- identify the deeper issues underlying a problem
- happily postpone decisions that are best left for a while

- pay painstaking attention to detail
- take a long-term view.

They can also:

- get hung up on unnecessary detail
- be dismissive of people who reach conclusions quickly, especially hares who they see as lightweights
- miss the boat with opportunities and fail to react to threats quickly enough
- hold up colleagues
- suffer from procrastination and paralysis of analysis
- fail to see the urgency of key decisions
- miss paradigm changes
- be indecisive.

In the same way, organizations tend to be hares or tortoises. From the quotation at the beginning of the chapter, for example, it is clear that Marks & Spencer sees its tortoise-like nature as a strength, even though others might perceive it as a dinosaur company, in danger of being left behind by more agile rivals. However, as David Clutterbuck and Walter Goldsmith point out in *The Winning Streak Mark II*, behind the calm exterior, M&S is a mass of continuous experimentation and modification. The world-famous retailer is, in effect, a cautious but deliberate decision-maker, balancing the need for change against the need to conserve core values.

Some companies, are hares. Again, this can be an advantage in a very fast-moving market.

Many other American and British companies, however, are 'time-driven' for no good reason, often looking at short-term horizons and placing great emphasis on tight schedules for their own sake. By contrast, many Japanese, German and Scandinavian companies in particular, tend to take a longer-term view and like M&S are more 'issues-driven'. When they make decisions, these companies see themselves as in it for the long haul.

As Michael Treschow, head of the Swedish engineering group Atlas Copco, explains:

'We are very, very persistent. People know that once we have decided something we are like a bulldozer, even if the bulldozer moves slow it means we're getting there.'

77

FAST IMPRESSIONS

Whether you are a hare or a tortoise, making an initial assessment of decisions allows you to immediately pigeon-hole them into one of a number of categories. While it is true that this practice comes more naturally to hares, it is a useful decision-making habit for tortoises to acquire.

Rather than allowing their concentration and efforts to be dissipated by thousands of unimportant tasks, in this way effective decision-makers pay attention to what is really important right now, but also consider decisions that will be important tomorrow or in six months' time.

PIGEON-HOLING DECISIONS

A useful way of categorizing decisions is in terms of the immediate action – or type of decision – that is required. From this perspective, decisions can be viewed as pieces of paper which come into a manager's in-tray and which require an initial assessment. In this way, it is possible to pigeon-hole the type of decision – or output required.

According to Roger Dawson,[1] there are at least four different pigeon-holes that decisions can fall into.

- **A right answer and a wrong answer:** this will usually apply to a decision which is based on concrete principles. Timing may be important but it will be necessary to gather the relevant information first. What is required immediately is to ensure that the collection of relevant data is undertaken quickly so that it does not hold up the decision-making process unnecessarily or render the decision obsolete.

- **Best option:** this is where the decision-maker is confronted by a number of alternatives and must decide between them on the best course of action. Again, a fast response may be important, but an effective decision demands that the alternatives be properly considered – otherwise there is no point in generating them.

- **No answer:** this applies to situations which have no immediate solution. These sorts of decisions are best put on the back burner. Making a decision for its own sake is pointless and may actually be detrimental.

- **'Go' or 'no go':** the only consideration with a 'go' or 'no go' decision is whether to go ahead with a course of action – be it a new project, a bid, or a management initiative – or not. Often, such decisions are sign-off situations, where a manager is asked to give a 'green light' to a proposal or recommendation.

Choosing a time-scale

The appropriate time-scale for making the decision should be dictated by the time-scales on which the course of action is based. If, for example, the proposal is to develop a new product or service to beat a competitor to market, the speed with which the decision-maker responds will have a direct impact on the feasibility of the project. In many organizations, however, by the time a project gets the green light it is unworkable within the designated deadline.

To Dawson's pigeon-holes, a number of others can be added. These include the following categories.

- **Act now decisions:** those which require an immediate response to exploit an opportunity or avoid a crisis. For example, a strike means a competitor will not be able to deliver on time presenting you with an opportunity that requires swift responses. Or, the account manager has learned that a key customer is thinking about switching to a supplier offering discounts and requires authorization to re-negotiate the price. In both cases the decision must be made quickly if it is to be effective.

- **'Go away' decisions:** these are decisions that, if they are not made immediately, will eventually go away. For example, a colleague relates the story of a decision to authorize an employee's new company car. Knowing full well that the man concerned would be leaving the company in less than a week, she said 'leave it with me'. By Friday he had received his P45 and the decision had 'gone away'.

- **'Not mine to make' decisions:** this applies to situations where a manager recognizes that he or she is not the right person to make a decision. Once this fact is recognized, the decision is to determine immediately who is – and either pass the decision down to someone closer to the issues, or up to someone with more authority or a clearer view of the big picture. (Correctly diagnosed, this is not the same as passing the buck, rather it is a sensible and responsible decision in its own right. However, sitting on the decision will be unproductive.)

- **Facilitating decisions:** faced with a particular decision, the manager recognizes that a general principle or policy decision is required which clarifies the position for others. By taking a bit more time to determine what the general policy should be, he or she will enable others to make quicker decisions in future. This is akin to unlocking doors. It answers the immediate need as well as ensuring similar decisions will not have to be referred back.

- **Re-framing decisions:** faced with a decision, a manager may decide that the wrong question is being asked, or that the goal-posts have moved. As such, the decision is to change the terms of reference. Again, this is a type of decision that requires some thought and probably some clarification. Simply throwing the issue back without an explanation will serve no useful purpose.

EVALUATING TIME-SCALES

What often prevents managers from evaluating the time-scales in this way, however, is their inability to manage their own time. As a consequence, there simply don't seem to be enough hours in a day to practise good decision-making habits. As a result, they tend to fall into one of three additional types.

- **Procrastinators:** tortoises by nature, these managers never get around to making a decision because they are too busy taking care of other aspects of their jobs. As a result, a backlog of decisions builds up which prevents them from making any decisions at all. Procrastinators shuffle pieces of paper – or decisions – around on their desks without coming to any conclusion.

- **Fire-fighters:** may be natural hares or tortoises. These managers put off decisions until the last possible moment (or sometimes later), and will only make a decision when the situation has already become critical. As a result, most of the decisions they make are made too late to prevent problems from developing.

- **Knee-jerkers:** hares through and through, managers in this group believe they are effective decision-makers because they make instant judgements on all decisions regardless of the time-scales involved. Because they jump to conclusions they are often more dangerous than either of the other two groups. Their ill-considered decisions cause havoc for those who have to try to implement unworkable or misguided initiatives. They often end up wasting a lot of time and resources on activities that later have to be curtailed.

Effective decision-makers, on the other hand, recognize that an important decision can have more value to the organization than countless routine tasks. One of the key skills required of senior managers is to separate out the important from the urgent, and to concentrate on what really matters. At any one time, this will probably mean focusing their firepower on as little as 20 per cent of their total workload. It also means understanding the difference between hard and soft deadlines.

Hard and soft deadlines

It pays to know whether a given date or hour is a hard deadline – the last possible moment at which the decision can be made – or a soft deadline – one that has a comfort factor built in to allow for slippage, or is simply being driven by a schedule that ought to be subservient to the decision.

The reason many managers don't distinguish between these two situations is because they are already trying to do too much in too few hours. As a result, they don't stop to think whether the decision should dictate the time-frame or the time-frame should dictate the decision.

Why, after all, base the entire future strategy of the company on the need to complete a report before the chief executive takes his holiday? But this is the sort of absurd situation that can arise.

Recognizing the drivers of a decision is an important aspect of effective decision-making. In itself, of course, this requires time for reflection and understanding of the pressures at play. This requires that most basic of management skills – good time management.

TIME MANAGEMENT

There are probably more books and courses on time management than any other aspect of management. But how many of us find the time to read or attend them? Today, the pressures on our time seem greater than ever. (This is ironic really, considering all the effort and money that has been invested this century in time-saving gadgets.)

In a recent article in the *Financial Times*,[2] Vanessa Houlder asks:

'Do you have a "do it now" policy? Do you aim to discriminate between urgent and important tasks? Do you wish you could prioritize your activities, hold "action centred" meetings and handle each piece of paper that arrives on your desk just once?

'If the answer is yes, the chances are that you are one of the millions of people who have studied time management – one of the best-known, yet least-applied, general management disciplines.'

How right she is. The problem is that no matter how snappy the phrases used by time management trainers, they only work if managers take the discipline seriously. Unfortunately, with the best will in the world, such aphorisms run into problems the moment most managers step out of the training session and back into the real world.

As a consequence, as Cathy Walton, a director at business psychologists Nicholson McBride, observes: 'Despite all the techniques there is a gap for most people between what's deeply important to them and the way they spend their time.'

When you consider, too, that an estimated 85 per cent of filed information is never looked at again, it becomes clear that one of the best – and simplest – time-saving gadgets ever invented is the wastepaper bin.

Management gridlock

In his book *Time Lock*, Ralph Keyes[3] describes a condition that is all too familiar to managers. He likens our current predicament to the time equivalent of gridlock on our roads. Our lives are so filled with things we **must do** or **should do**, let alone the things we **want to do**, that we feel trapped.

More than that, in our working lives many of us feel under increasing pressure, with the threat of redundancy hanging over us like the executioner's axe. If there is an adage that seems to fit the 1990s it is that 'no-one is indispensable'.

Hyrum W Smith's ten natural laws

The American author and time management expert Hyrum W Smith describes how many managers feel today.

'Life is getting more and more hectic. The daily treadmill is accelerating, and we have to run faster and faster just to stay in one place. The demands of the competitive marketplace put such a premium on personal productivity that, if you're not productive, you're out. The result is a tremendous pressure to perform, coupled with a sense of overwhelming insecurity about the future.'[4]

No wonder, then, that decisions don't get the timely attention they require. But according to Smith, whose company the Franklin Quest provides time management training to some of America's leading companies, managers can manage their time more effectively if they take the time to understand and follow ten natural laws.

▶

> Several of Smith's ten laws are directly applicable to decision-making.
>
> For example:
>
> - **determining the highest priorities**
> - **learning to differentiate between urgent and vital tasks**
> - **re-evaluating which events you can and cannot control**
> - **getting rid of 'time robbers'.**
>
> Of these, the last is perhaps the easiest to recognize but also the hardest to tackle.

Banishing the 'time bandits'

You may remember the film *The Time Bandits* with John Cleese and some of his Monty Python colleagues. All of us suffer from time bandits in our working lives. One of the most important decision-making habits is learning to make space for important decisions, and that involves recognizing and eliminating time bandits.

The popular image of the high-powered executive, reinforced by dozens of Hollywood movies, is the man surrounded by an entourage of personal assistants and subordinates. These minions frantically scribble down snap decisions made off the top of his head as he strides purposefully from meeting to meeting. This is, of course, a caricature. But as with all the best caricatures there is a large grain of truth in it. Too many managers make decisions on the hoof because they do not create the space in their schedules to give the issues the attention they deserve.

One reason for this is the way that business life is organized. There is a whole range of time-wasting conventions and bad habits that impinge on our working days, all of which can steal the time that could be better allocated to effective decision-making.

Smith names no fewer than 32 of these 'time robbers' – most of them instantly recognizable to any manager. He categorizes them as Group A – those imposed on us; and Group B – self-inflicted (see box).

Effective decision-makers find ways to banish the time bandits long enough to create the space they need to make decisions. To do that, they first have to understand the time-scales involved.

One other thing. Holding and creating time to think and make decisions while all around you are running around like headless chickens is

83

Time robbers

Among the time robbers Hyrum Smith lists in **Group A** are:

- unclear job definitions
- unnecessary meetings
- too much work
- poor communication
- equipment failure
- disorganized boss

- red tape
- conflicting priorities
- untrained staff
- lack of authority
- mistakes of others
- revised deadlines.

And in **Group B**:

- failure to delegate
- failure to listen
- fatigue
- socializing
- paper shuffling

- cluttered workspace – waste time looking for things
- perfectionism
- attempting too much – the hero or martyr syndrome.
- indecision.

not easy. Nor does it happen naturally. Like most aspects of management, it is a discipline which has to be learned, often the hard way.

But show me a senior manager with no blank slots in his diary and I'll show you a company where decisions don't get the attention they deserve.

Just because it's urgent, doesn't mean it's vital

As Hyrum Smith points out, there is an important distinction to be made between vital and urgent tasks. But all too often, a vital decision gets put off because an urgent task steals the time that we have set aside to make it. Because of the way we work, too, there is a bias towards tasks that require our immediate attention.

As Smith says:

'An urgent task is something that demands immediate attention. It comes out of left field and says: "Hey, I need to be done right now." By far the most common is the telephone. Every time your telephone rings, what is it saying to you? "Pick me up, pick me up,

pick me up". You don't go around picking up phones unless they are ringing, and the only thing the ring says is, "I want to be dealt with right now". But are most phone calls important? One or two a day, perhaps, but not the vast majority. Would you like to feel some real power today? Let the phone ring!'

But how many of us heed his excellent advice? Not many. In part, this is because we know that we will only have to return the call later so it is better to deal with the matter now rather than have it hanging over us. Besides, it might be one of those two important calls.

As a result, a strategic decision that is vital to the success or even survival of the business is put on the back burner while we deal with a stationery order, make lunch arrangements or juggle our diaries to fit in a meeting that we know is a waste of time for all concerned. And so it goes on, and the vital decision is delayed for weeks or even months until a crisis develops.

One way that decision-makers can ensure their time is effectively spent is to realize that a small percentage of decisions account for a large percentage of results. This phenomenon gives rise to the 80/20 principle.

THE 80/20 PRINCIPLE

This is the name that Richard Koch,[5] consultant turned management writer, has given to what he believes is an underlying principle of human activity. Namely, that 80 per cent of results flow from just 20 per cent of the causes. The 80/20 principle, argues Koch in his book of the same name, is the one true principle of highly effective people and organizations.

> 'One way that decision-makers can ensure their time is effectively spent is to realize that a small percentage of decisions account for a large percentage of results.'

According to Koch, the main tenets of the 80/20 principle are as follows.

- The doctrine of the vital few and the trivial many: there are only a few things that ever produce important results.
- Most efforts do not realize their intended results.
- What you see is generally not what you get: there are subterranean forces at work.
- It is usually too complicated and too wearisome to work out what is happening and it is also unnecessary: all you need to know is whether something is working or not and change the mix until it is; then keep the mix constant until it stops working.

- Most good events happen because of a small minority of highly productive forces; most bad things happen because of a few highly destructive forces.

- Most activity, *en masse* and individually, is a waste of time. It will not contribute materially to desired results.

From these, he says, five lessons – or rules – can be drawn for decision-making.

- **Rule 1:** says that not many decisions are very important. Remember that only one in 20 is likely to be important. Do not agonize over the unimportant decisions and, above all, do not conduct expensive and time-consuming analysis. If possible delegate them all.

- **Rule 2:** affirms that the most important decisions are often made by default, because turning points have come and gone without being recognized. For example, key members of staff leave; competitors develop new products, or you lose a leading market-share position because the distribution channels change. When this happens, Koch says, no amount of data gathering will help. What is needed is intuition and insight.

- **Rule 3:** the 80/20 principle is for important decisions: gather 80 per cent of the data and perform 80 per cent of the analysis in the first 20 per cent of the time available, then make a decision 100 per cent of the time and act as if you were 100 per cent confident of that decision. Koch calls this 'the 80/20/100/100 rule of decision-taking'.

- **Rule 4:** if what you have decided isn't working, change your mind early rather than late. The market is a more reliable indicator than any amount of analysis. Don't be afraid to experiment. And don't try to fight the market if something isn't working.

- **Rule 5:** when something is working really well, double and redouble your bets. This is the 20 per cent of really productive forces working in your favour, so capitalize on it.

Koch's advice is at the same time both simple and deceptively difficult to apply, but a great many managers would be much more effective if they tried to follow it. The way most executives conduct their working lives, however, they are more likely to fall into the Catch 23 trap than unleash the power of the 80/20 principle.

Catch 23

Management writer Edward de Bono[6] coined the phrase 'Catch 23' for a phenomenon in management that has important implications for decision-making. Basically, it goes as follows: 'It is essential that something gets done, but it never makes sense to do it at any particular moment'. In other words, managers have a tendency to put off really important and often difficult decisions because they believe that events don't move so quickly that they require an immediate reaction. Rather, they prefer to postpone the painful decision until a more appropriate time. This often goes on until it really is too late and what is required is crisis management.

CRISIS? WHAT CRISIS?

Crises are perhaps the most clearcut examples of a situation where decisions are both urgent and vital. In fact, the word crisis originates from the Greek, *krinein*, to decide. A company crisis therefore is a decisive moment, a time of great difficulty or danger in a company's history.

So profoundly threatening are crises in corporate life that a whole area of management theory and a £multi-million business has grown up around them called 'crisis management'. Often, though the seeds of crisis lie in the indecisiveness of senior managers.

Consultant Lex Van Gunsteren[7] has written widely on the subject. He observes:

'Crises are commonplace in management. Yet, the same mistakes in handling them are made repeatedly. Indifferent or complacent managers remain in their positions for too long. Owners may appear to be loathe to change a once successful management team and managers with crisis management skills are brought in too late.

'Similarly, the signs of impending crisis are routinely overlooked as commentators, analysts, investors and managers concentrate on hard financial data rather than the soft data which points to other conclusions.'

Van Gunsteren distinguishes between two types of company crisis:

- unpleasant surprise crisis
- management crisis.

An unpleasant surprise crisis, he says, can happen to any company. A product may unexpectedly have a quality problem; a war may break out in a country that is a key market for the company; or a world crisis – such as the Gulf War – may profoundly affect an industry such as airlines, travel agencies and hotels.

A management crisis, on the other hand, rarely comes as a complete surprise to insiders. Often employees further down the organization can see it coming long before the top team admits there is serious problem.

Van Gunsteren notes:

'The saying "When you do not make a profit, you are either in the wrong business or have the wrong management" is only true in the short term. Being in the wrong business is a failure of management: it did not change the scope of the business at the right time. So, if a business consistently fails to make a profit it simply has the wrong management.'

The last thing that a crisis-torn management will do, however, is admit its own incompetence. As Van Gunsteren observes:

'Failing management always blames external circumstances, conveniently forgetting that "a collapse of the market", "unfair competition from low-wage countries", "competition from substitute products", etc. do not suddenly emerge, but can be foreseen and anticipated.'

When a crisis is caused by a failure in management decision-making, however, it is usually because of changes in circumstances which mean that the old formulas no longer work. According to Van Gunsteren, when management is the cause of the crisis, two factors usually prevail.

1. Arrogance through success, resulting in:
   - less willingness to learn or adjust
   - ego tripping: a need to be in the limelight which makes the manager more oriented towards himself than towards the business
   - an urge to leave a monument behind as a 'crown on his career'
   - fear of losing face.

2. The effect of the manager's lifecycle. The manager's energy has declined, as has his feeling for the market. He may have lost contact with the company's environment, primarily because his external contacts are based on old relationships. In this situation, often the manager is no longer aware of modern techniques, nor is he prepared to make a serious effort to develop essential new skills. As a result, he is concerned with preserving the *status quo*, and does not want to take any risks that might involve failing.

Van Gunsteren also notes that when the problem lies with the chief executive a number of other symptoms can usually be observed: one of which is indecisiveness. This, he suggests, is the best indication of an impending crisis, and is the time to bring in new management.

Crisis management

Managing a crisis situation requires a special set of skills. A crisis usually requires a quick reaction from the organization. Usually, this will involve very fast decision-making.

A growing number of specialist consultancies and other expert trouble-shooters offer crisis management services to companies. Often, they are most useful in putting policies and procedures in place which allow companies to react rapidly when faced with a crisis. In fact, the most important decision affecting the outcome of a crisis will often be one made months or even years before to train the necessary people in crisis management and to have a plan in place. The plan creates a default decision process for handling the critical first few hours – i.e., if this happens then we automatically know to do this.

CASE STUDY: THE TYLENOL SCARE

To many, the classic example of cool decision-making under pressure was that made by Johnson & Johnson when faced with product tampering of its painkiller Tylenol. Badly handled, the sabotage could have ruined the Tylenol brand image, and even done irreparable damage to the company.

What senior managers at Johnson & Johnson did, however, was to instantly put themselves in the public's shoes. They acted decisively, immediately pulling all Tylenol products off the shelves, and supporting the decision with endless press conferences to keep the public informed. In so doing, they sacrificed the short-term cost and loss of sales to protect both the integrity of the product and equally importantly the reputation of the company.

Subsequent market research showed that the decisive handling of the crisis led to greater customer loyalty in the long run. Moreover, they also made a decision to take steps to ensure that the situation was not repeated by developing a tamper-proof capsule which offered protection in future.

CASE STUDY: HOOVER

However, there are also many examples of disastrous decision-making in a crisis. Take the misguided marketing promotion by Hoover a few years back, for example. What seemed at first a brilliant idea to boost sales – by offering two free flights to Europe or the US to any UK customer who spent a minimum of £100 on Hoover products – turned into a corporate disaster because marketing executives miscalculated the strength of consumer tenacity, making the promotion much more expensive than anticipated.

The problem was brought to light not by managers, who must have known that complaints were mounting, but by media stories of angry customers who bought Hoover products, filled out their applications for tickets and then heard nothing from the company. The first mistake was then exacerbated by a series of subsequent blunders. These included a failure to act quickly enough to restore customer confidence and a public relations *faux pas* involving a comment from a Hoover manager that customers were foolish to expect something for nothing.

In April 1993, Hoover's US parent company Maytag announced a net loss of $10.5 million (£7 million) in the first quarter, after taking a special charge of $30 million to cover the unexpected cost of the promotion.

FASTER, HARDER

As well as the traditional time pressures, a number of new developments are also changing the pattern and speed of business decision-making beyond all recognition.

The first and most significant change is the arrival of information technology which allows people anywhere in the world to communicate much more quickly. The other major influence is the ever-accelerating pace of change in the business world. These two phenomena are closely linked, and feed off one another. The ability to communicate almost instantly with any part of the world is driving the creation of a global marketplace. This in turn makes speed of response to market demands a key element of competitive power.

The impact of IT on the way we do our jobs can be gauged from recent research. It confirms that we now spend more of our working lives in front of computer screens than ever before. Not only does the omnipresent PC (or Mac) dominate our desks, increasingly it dominates our lives, including the way we communicate – and increasingly the way we make decisions.

The findings, from what is claimed to be the first ever worldwide computer census, indicate that UK office workers now spend almost half (48 per cent) of their working lives peering at a flickering screen – that's a 15 per cent increase since 1993. US workers are even more dependent than their UK counterparts, spending 67 per cent of each working day at their terminals.

Sponsored by the management consultancy Compass, the research was conducted by Kit Grindley, Price Waterhouse professor of systems automation at the London School of Economics.[8] According to Professor Grindley, it wasn't until 1993 that computers really began to dominate our lives. 'Office culture has changed as a result', he says.

'In the short space of three years, traditional secretaries, with a monopoly control of communication channels, are now giving way to groupware systems which allow direct communication between decision-makers, work teams and information sources. And office supervisors are being replaced by screen-based progress trackers.'

At the same time, some 57 per cent of all external communications now rely on information technology, dramatically changing the way that businesses interact with customers and suppliers.

'IT is showing a considerable influence on the traditional boundary communications between companies, their suppliers and customers', says Professor Grindley.

As one IT director in the survey put it:

'Electronic commerce does more than spell doom for the postman because it is more than a new way of communication. The fact that anyone, anywhere, anytime can be communicating, lifts the old restrictions which confined business to centralized offices controlling do-it-all factories. Anyone can make your product, and any place will do as an "office desk".'

E-mail and snail mail

Crude by the standards of some of today's groupware, e-mail is nevertheless one of the most widely used forms of electronic communication. It allows messages to be sent directly from one computer terminal to another without so much as picking up the telephone.

Fans boast about the speed of e-mail compared to traditional post – which they disparagingly refer to as 'snail mail'. However, some commentators say the full impact of this and other forms of communication made possible by IT is only now becoming apparent.

Graeme Hoyle, a consultant trainer for Reed Personnel, says that although many senior managers don't understand the new technology, e-mail has the power to break down traditional hierarchies by enabling people at any level and any geographical location to talk to each other and make decisions.

In more traditional companies, e-mail often just duplicates the traditional hierarchy, Hoyle says, with messages sent up the line to bosses who then pass them on to their bosses or send them back down again to the person who will actually carry out the work.

Hoyle agrees that e-mail can lead to greater democracy, but only if the culture of the company permits. *'It can either be seen as the best thing since sliced bread or it can be seen as subversive, it depends on the organization.'*

The impact of IT is a significant factor in the increasing pressure on companies to react more quickly to anticipate customer needs. This translates into shorter product lifecycles and a need for faster decision-making to bring new products to market in less time. Many commentators believe that agility and speed of response is now a key source of competitive advantage.

THE NIMBLE ORGANIZATION

The origins of this idea date back to a book written by Rosabeth Moss Kanter, *When Giants Learn to Dance*,[9] and another by James A Belasco called *Teaching the Elephant to Dance*,[10] both of which argued that large corporations could only survive if they found ways to overcome their bureaucratic inertia.

Richard Pascale, management academic and writer, also advocates the concept of the 'agile organization'. In an interview with Godfrey Golzen, editor of *Human Resources* magazine (March/April 1997), for example, Pascale suggests that agility could become the next business buzzword.[11]

And in his typical forthright manner, management guru Tom Peters recently declared: 'Agility is the core competence of the future.'

In fact, speed of decision-making as a competitive advantage is a strand that runs through much of Peters' writing over the past decade.

Support for these ideas comes from a prize-winning *California Management Review* article by Stanford professor Kathleen Eisenhardt. Entitled 'Speed and strategic choice: How managers accelerate decision-making', the article draws on the author's study (with University of Virginia colleague Jay Bourgeois) of decision-makers in 12 computer firms in Silicon Valley.[12]

They found that the slower companies took 12 to 18 months to achieve what the faster companies managed in just 2 to 4 months.

In the article, Eisenhardt highlights five major distinctions between the two groups.

1. The fast decision-makers swam in a deep, turbulent sea of real-time information; while the slower ones relied on planning and futuristic information.

2. The fast decision-makers tracked a few key operating measures such as bookings, cash and engineering milestones, often updating them daily and scheduling as many as three weekly top management meetings to understand 'what's happening'. They also used a constant e-mail dialogue and face-to-face discussions, rather than the memos and lengthy reports that typified the slow decision-makers.

3. The slow decision-makers also considered fewer alternatives than their faster counterparts, and minutely dissected each alternative while the greyhounds considered batches of options at the same time.

4. The slow coaches were 'stymied by conflict', with constant delays; whereas the bullets thrived on conflict, which they saw as a natural and desirable part of the process, but the senior decision-maker was also prepared to step in if needed and make a decision. These companies also relied on 'an older and more experienced' mentor for advice, whereas the slow decision-makers had no such advisers.

5. Finally, says Eisenhardt, the fast kids thoroughly integrated strategies and tactics, juggling budgets, schedules, and options simultaneously. The slow kids examined strategy in a vacuum, and were more likely to trip over details on implementing decisions.

The way that the faster decision-makers operated Eisenhardt character-ized as 'all at once' behaviour. In recent years a number of new organizations have demonstrated that the speed of decision-making is greatly enhanced when activities are carried out 'all at once'. One notable example is the 24-hour news channel CNN, which set up its operation from scratch in a matter of months and has continued to lead the way in many areas of broadcasting. CNN prides itself on the speed with which it can react to news breaking in any corner of the globe.

Less haste, more speed

Despite these examples of rapid decision-making, as the old adage sug-gests, there is a paradox at the heart of how many decisions are made. Often, a tight schedule will drive important decisions rather than the other way round. To some extent, the way that Western companies are run can actually prevent managers from achieving their goals. Many organizations seem more concerned about creating the appearance of progress than making real progress.

For one thing, inordinate amounts of time are wasted in meetings which should have been cancelled because there is insufficient clarity or information to make the decisions that need to be taken What tends to happen, however, is that the decisions are made anyway, and the orga-nization moves on to the next phase of the project. Japanese companies, as we will see in Chapter 7, do things differently.

JUST-IN-TIME DECISIONS

One way to think about decision-making in the new era is to liken it to the just-in-time production systems pioneered by Japanese companies and since adopted by many Western manufacturers.

JIT grew out of the recognition that production – assembly lines in particular – required an unbroken supply of components, which took up large amounts of space and involved expensive inventory. Japanese companies therefore developed a different approach. They recognized that if materials, components and products are produced for, or deliv-ered to, the next stage of production at the exact time they are needed, then the amount of inventory laying around at the factory or held by the company could be minimized.

A good example of JIT at work is the way that a number of car man-ufacturers now operate. By standardizing components they have reached a point where each individual car can be built to order. In other words, it is produced only when an order has been placed for it. In this way, rather than produce hundreds of cars in each colour and each specification, the exact requirements of the final customer are known in advance so that each car that rolls off the assembly line is built to the specifications of the customer who ordered it. The reduction in wastage is huge.

Decision-making can also be viewed in this way. Rather than a bunch of solutions chasing problems – which is what has tended to happen with many organizations in the past – decisions should be made when and where the need arises, and should be prompted not by internal processes but by the demands of customers in the market. Quite simply, it is both time-consuming and pointless to refer a decision up the chain of command if it

> '... decisions should be made when and where the need arises, and should be prompted not by internal processes but by the demands of customers in the market.'

can be resolved on the spot. And any decision that doesn't flow directly from the market is probably a waste of time anyway.

References

1. Dawson, Roger, *Make the Right Decision Every Time*, Nicholas Brealey, 1993.

2. Houlder, V, 'Ticking over efficiently', *Financial Times*, 17 February 1997.

3. Keyes, R, *Time Lock*.

4. Smith, Hyrum W, *The 10 Laws of Successful Time and Life Management*, Nicholas Brealey, 1994.

5. Koch, Richard, *The 80/20 Principle*, Nicholas Brealey, 1997.

6. de Bono, E, *Future Positive*, Penguin, 1983.

7. Van Gunsteren, Lex, *FT Handbook of Management 1995*.

8. Grindley, K, *International Computer Census*, Compass.

9. Kanter, R M, *When Giants Learn to Dance*, Simon & Schuster, 1980.

10. Belasco, James A, *Teaching the Elephant to Dance*, Century, 1990.

11. Golzen, Godfrey, 'The Next Big Idea', *Human Resources*, March/April 1997.

12. Eisenhardt, Kathleen, 'Speed and Strategic Choice: How managers accelerate decision-making', *California Management Review*, Winter 1989, Vol. 89, No.2.

Data, data everywhere

'Companies want to empower their knowledge workers with information to make decisions. It is the lifeblood of a company.'
BILL GATES, CEO Microsoft

'Information is not knowledge until it has been processed by the human mind.'
DR DAVID LEWIS, occupational psychologist

Just as we saw with timing in the last chapter, when it comes to the information that decisions are based on, there is a balance to be struck between too much and too little data. Some decisions require careful research and analysis. But too much research can lead to procrastination and a paralysis of analysis, resulting in costly delays.

There is an important distinction to be drawn, too, between quantity and quality of data. This chapter looks at:

- information vs knowledge
- the right information for making a decision
- information drift (factors that can make decision-makers drift off course)
- reliability of information
- Chinese whispers (good news goes up, bad news comes down)
- testing for bias
- Cassandra information (key data that is overlooked)
- information flow
- benchmarking
- information overload
- developing good information habits
- desktop democratization
- paralysis by analysis.

INFORMATION VS KNOWLEDGE

Before looking at the issues, there is another point that needs to be made. Information is not the same thing as knowledge. One way to think about this is to regard data or information as the raw material which goes into the human brain and knowledge as the product of that information once it has been digested by the mental processes. This is not a precise definition, of course, but it does at least distinguish the two.

(Scientists are still struggling to understand exactly what constitutes knowledge. Most agree, however, that several factors are at work in the conversion of data to usable knowledge. One of those factors appears to be experience. Another is the degree of interest and understanding that the individual invests in the process. Some management commentators claim that we have now moved from the 'information age' to the 'knowledge age', but most are equally vague about what this really means.)

Data for data's sake

One of the biggest flaws in the way decisions are made is the failure to identify not just how much information is needed to make an effective decision but what constitutes the right information. As a result, for every manager making a decision based on insufficient data there is another who gathers too much information or the wrong information.

There is no simple answer to this dilemma. In most cases it requires the decision-maker to make a judgement. But there are some simple questions which form part of what can be described as good decision-making habits. Many of these questions are so basic that they seem unnecessary. Yet many of even the most rudimentary points are regularly ignored.

Remember, information is one of the key inputs into the decision-making process. The quality of what is input has direct consequences for the quality of the output. Or, to borrow from computer speak: 'rubbish in, rubbish out'. The best process in the world will struggle to make a silk purse from a sow's ear.

DO YOU HAVE THE RIGHT INFORMATION TO MAKE A DECISION?

One of the first questions a decision-maker should ask is: 'What information do I need to make this decision?' It sounds obvious, but what often happens is that managers start from a different perspective altogether. The question they ask (if they ask a question at all) is: 'What information do I have to make this decision?'

This is a classic case of putting the cart before the horse. Take the example of a manager deciding whether to launch a new product in Japan. He may have all sorts of information about con-

> '... information is one of the key inputs into the decision-making process. The quality of what is input has direct consequences for the quality of the output.'

sumer tastes and buying habits in the US and in Europe. He may have some good data on the costs of exporting the product to Tokyo. He may even have Japanese friends who think it's a sure-fire winner. Yet he lacks the one piece of information that he most needs – namely what Japanese consumers think about his product.

Ridiculous as it sounds, this is what a great many of us do when we make important decisions. (A variation on the theme is where the manager asks someone else to gather the missing information, or tries to collect it himself. Two weeks and a lot of frustrating research later, what has been collected is some excellent data about the consumer tastes of people in Hong Kong, Australia and Hawaii but precious little on Japan. The manager then decides that this will have to do and bases his decision on it.)

Interrogate the problem

The best way to get around this problem is to prioritize information. This is a vital element of developing good decision-making habits. To borrow from journalism, there will usually be three types of information:

- need to know information (must have)
- nice to know information (useful background)
- and irrelevant information (interesting or not, of no use for this decision).

Identifying which data falls into these categories can best be achieved by interrogating the problem. Questions that should be addressed, for example, include the following.

- What are the key success criteria for this decision? (Sales in Japan exceeding x would probably be one in the example above.)
- What could go wrong?
- What impact will it have if it does?

In this way, it is possible to very quickly arrive at a better understanding of the information required to make the decision.

Developing these sorts of information habits will also mean that information gathering is a much more targeted process, rather than simply trying to assimilate all the available information on a particular topic. To some extent, too, it may involve teasing out data that is not readily available. Once the parameters have been set, though, the information-gathering process can begin.

An analogy here is the comparison between the fly fisherman who knows precisely what he is fishing for and will use his skill to bring the trout to the surface; and the skipper of the trawler who simply looks through his nets to see what he's caught. Both can be effective of course, but one requires a lot more time and resources. As more and more information becomes available, the trawler model becomes less and less attractive.

It is also useful to consider what can go wrong at the information-gathering stage. Once again, it is by better understanding the flaws in the way human beings operate that we can become more effective decision-makers. One of the most important factors here is the effects of a phenomenon that can be called information drift (see box).

Information drift

Roger Dawson,[1] the American management author, identifies eight factors in the information-gathering process that can make decision-makers drift off course and reduce the effectiveness of the resulting decisions. These are:

- availability drift
- experience drift
- conflict drift
- recall drift

- selectivity drift
- anchoring drift
- recency drift
- favourability drift.

Some of these touch on points covered later, but any one of the eight can cloud the judgement of a decision-maker by causing him or her to drift off course. In particular, information drift can lead to decisions which are based on inaccurate information, or can result in important opportunities being overlooked.

The eight drifts can be summarized as follows.

- **Availability drift:** is when the decision-maker gives more weight to information that's readily available. (This is the 'what information do I have?' rather than 'what information do I need?' problem. In other words, the more you are aware of something, the more likely you are to give it emphasis it doesn't deserve.)

- **Experience drift:** people tend to see things in terms of their own personal or professional interest. If you are a horse-racing fan you tend to think it's the most popular sport in the world. Similarly, a human resources manager will have a tendency to see the HR dimensions of a problem or decision as the most important consideration; an accountant may see it differently.

- **Conflict drift:** human beings have a natural tendency to reject information which conflicts with their own beliefs. A decision-maker, then, is likely to ignore information which contradicts his or her preferred solution.

- **Recall drift:** people are better at recalling information about topics which are familiar to them. They are not so good at recalling data from areas where they have no expertise.

▶
- **Selectivity drift:** because human beings are unable to absorb everything, they tend to filter out information and observations about issues that do not interest them.

- **Anchoring drift:** if you are not an expert in a particular area, there is a tendency to latch on to the first information that comes to light, or the opinion of the first 'expert' consulted.

- **Recency drift:** we all have a tendency to place greater emphasis on what has just happened to us. We may also be inclined to place more trust in recent information even though analysis carried out some time ago was more thorough.

- **Favourability drift:** people have a tendency to look harder for information that supports their own beliefs or views than to actively seek out data that contradicts them.

Understanding and recognizing these potential drifts is the best protection against them.

The next part of this chapter looks at another important decision-making habit – interrogating the data itself.

HOW RELIABLE IS THE INFORMATION?

The weight we attach to a piece of information depends on a number of factors, including the reliability of the source. (Here we deal with external sources, internal sources are considered later.) For example, how you would react to the results of a study on the effects of smoking might vary depending on whether it was funded by:

1. an anti-smoking organization
2. a tobacco company
3. an independent medical research institution.

A useful exercise here is to interrogate a newspaper or magazine article. The tools for this are a simple set of questions.

- Who?
- What?
- Why?

103

- Where?
- When?
- How?

With these it should be possible to extract the information content from any source. Take our earlier piece of research, for example.

- Who carried out the research? Who paid for it?
- What were the researchers trying to do? Were they asking the right questions of the right people?
- Why? Is it an objective view or are there any vested interests involved? What premise or hypothesis were they trying to support or demolish?
- Where was it conducted? Europe, US, Africa? Worldwide? Does that make it more or less applicable to here?
- When was it carried out? Was it done last month? Last year? Ten years ago? Is it out of date?
- How was the study conducted? Was it based on a large or small sample? Telephone interviews or face-to-face? Were respondents anonymous? Does this make it more or less reliable?

Most of us do some sort of interrogation like this every time we read something (certainly we should). But developing the habit allows information to be assessed and often discarded much more rapidly. This is becoming increasingly important for a number of reasons. One of these is the enormous variety of informational sources now available. Another is the sheer volume of data they provide (something discussed under *Information overload* later in this chapter).

So much for external sources. But internal sources also require careful handling.

CHINESE WHISPERS

A factor to be borne in mind when assessing information from sources inside the organization is a phenomenon that we are all familiar with. Put simply, it is the tendency for organizations to filter information as it passes through. In particular, there is a tendency for bad news to be filtered out as information moves up through the organization, while good news is accentuated in the telling: good news goes up, bad news comes down. We've all done it, and most of us continue to do it.

What happens is that information we receive from below is adjusted slightly to make it more palatable to our boss, and make us appear in a more favourable light. Usually, this involves little more than rounding up the pluses and rounding down the minuses. It's usually fairly harmless, but the cumulative effect of these 'Chinese whispers' can actually distort the information that senior managers base their decisions on.

So, for example, take an update of progress on an important report. The manager responsible hasn't started writing it yet because he's had too many other issues to deal with. But he can't tell his boss that, so he reports 'a good start'. His boss, when asked by the next level of management, does the same, interpreting the first message as 'coming along', which is then reported as 'well underway', which then becomes 'excellent progress' and ends up by the time it reaches the board as 'putting the finishing touches to'.

The same thing has been known to happen with figures. A 46 per cent success rate for a new system can easily get rounded up to a 50 per cent success rate, which is then interpreted as over half, which becomes well over half, and eventually ends up as 'upper quartile'.

The exact reverse happens with the flow of information down an organization. Each manager in the reporting line adds his or her own criticisms to those of their bosses. The result is that a gentle rebuke from the chief executive can result in someone further down the organization being bawled out.

CULTURE CHANGE AT ROVER

These facts of corporate life make it essential to evaluate where information is coming from. In particular, it is useful to understand any potential biases and other factors that might be at play. A good example came from John Towers, former chief executive of Rover Cars.

Discussing the culture change that had occurred at Rover in the 1980s, he explained the way things used to work in the bad old days of British Leyland. In particular, he described a culture where, if senior managers were asked a question, rather than admit that the relevant information would have to be collected from fact-holders lower down, they would provide off-the-cuff input into important decisions. This Towers quickly rectified. As he explained:

►

▶

'Before, at the point where the facts were available there was no authority. The "fact-holders" themselves had very little opportunity to get involved with the decision-making, while at senior-level meetings, questions were being answered that it shouldn't have been possible to answer without consulting the fact-holders. These answers were then being fed into the decision-making process, so we were making important decisions based on opinions and subjective views. That's no way to run a business.'

He's right, of course, but there are many companies that still suffer from this problem.

There are also a great many where internal politics and career manoeuvring results in individuals putting their own spin on the facts. The best safeguard against this is to test the source of the data for bias.

TESTING FOR BIAS

Information drift is often exacerbated, Dawson says, where others are feeding data into the process. Under these circumstances, a number of questions can be used to evaluate the information provided by others.

1. Does the person giving me this information have a personal stake in this decision? Is he or she consciously or unconsciously trying to sway my opinion?

2. Does the person gathering this information have a reasonable amount of expertise in this area?

3. How much time did this person have to put the data together? Is there a danger that time pressure has led to superficial reporting or short cuts?

4. Does the person presenting this information have a prejudice of one kind or another? (He or she may not have a personal stake in the decision, but may have a bias in one direction or another. For example, is the person more or less risk-averse than you? Does he or she have a prejudice for or against technology, or moving into overseas markets?)

5. How does this data reflect on the individual providing it? Does it make him or his department look good or bad?

No-one is suggesting that colleagues should be interrogated before the data they provide is accepted. Rather, the effective decision-maker is someone who is aware of potential bias and compensates for it when reaching a conclusion.

An excellent example of this is provided by Sir Clive Thompson, chief executive of Rentokill Initial. Asked what he regarded as the single most important piece of information for managing the business, he replied:[2]

> 'If I went into a new company tomorrow it would probably be a different answer, but because I know this company so well, I short cut an enormous amount of information. I receive a forecast from every manager for the year (it's very important to have a full breakdown as consolidated forecasts can be misleading). These are reviewed each month. Because I know the individual managers – which ones are optimists and which are pessimists – I know from those forecasts what the profit will be for the year.'

What Thompson is doing, then, is interpreting data based on what he knows about the manager providing it, in order to gain a clearer picture of the company's overall performance.

This also highlights the dangers of consolidated information. Accountants know that combining good and bad figures often results in levelling out of the highs and the lows. This can result in less experienced managers failing to see important signposts. It also raises the issue of what management writer and consultant Lex Van Gunsteren calls 'Cassandra information'.

CASSANDRA INFORMATION

Van Gunsteren identifies a type of information that can affect senior managers and which he calls 'Cassandra information'.[3] Of the information that comes to the attention of directors, he says, only a part is relevant for the fulfilment of their tasks. That information can be called **'used information'** – it is both relevant and heeded.

Other information, which is not relevant but nevertheless receives attention, he calls **'confusion information'**, because covering irrelevant details results in confusion about the issue at hand.

Conversely, a third category of data – **'Cassandra information'** – goes unheeded. This is information which is at the heart of the issue but does not get the attention it should: key data that is overlooked.

Cassandra information takes its name from the classic story of the god Apollo, who having fallen in love with Cassandra, the beautiful daughter of King Priam of Troy, gave her the gift of being able to predict the future. When she spurned his attentions despite the present, he could not take back his gift – as a gift from a god is forever. Therefore, he bestowed on her a second attribute – that no-one would ever listen to her. This meant that when she warned the Trojans about the wooden horse, her advice was ignored and the city was subsequently destroyed.

According to Van Gunsteren, the causes of Cassandra information are:

- the information is not sufficiently accessible to decision-makers
- the information is too threatening – (the information that the war with the Greeks wasn't over, for example, was too threatening for the Trojans so they dismissed it).

The moral of the story for decision-makers is clear. Beware Cassandra information: it is often the first warning that an issue is becoming urgent.

INFORMATION FLOW

According to management author David Clutterbuck there are three key types of information flow.[4] These are:

- task information
- context information
- motivational information.

All three can have relevance for decision-makers. It is important, however, to understand which is being sought and which received.

- **Task information:** what people need to know to do their jobs. When job-holders themselves define this information, it is in very different terms than those used by senior managers. For example, the front-line employee might place much greater emphasis than his or her manager on having as much data as possible on the previous transaction history of individual customers.

  Task information takes three main forms. One is the basic data about the job – its specifications and any relevant background information. One is relevant feedback, which must be timely, accurate and presented in a way that is convenient to use. And the third relates to improvement in skills and knowledge that can be applied to the job – this includes training materials.

- **Context information:** what the individual needs to know to see how his or her tasks and decisions fit into the broader picture. Context information can include the vision or mission statement, information about the industry sector, meetings between directors and managers to explain business strategy and so on. Context information is vital to ensure that people see their job as part of a larger whole. Without it, managers make decisions in a vacuum.

A good example of a company providing context information is Ford in its new plant at Bridgend. The company agreed with unions to make all business information available to employees as part of the company's plan to end the age-old antagonism between trade unions and management. A union representative was reported as commenting that the management/union team at the Bridgend plant shared one objective that the plant should prosper.

- **Motivational information:** information the individual needs to feel that his or her efforts are appreciated. Motivational information needs to be fine-tuned to the needs of individuals and teams. It also tends to work best, the closer to the recipient it originates. Recognition from head office, for example, may be of less motivational impact than peer recognition, and will certainly involve a much longer interval between cause and effect. Decision-makers in particular should look for signs that they have the support and confidence of senior management. Without it, ambitious decisions are unlikely to have the commitment necessary to succeed.

BENCHMARKING

One of the biggest problems for organizations is knowing how they compare with others. In many cases, decisions about performance improvement require quantification if they are to be effective. It is of little use, for example, simply deciding that production wastage levels, or delivery times have to be improved if you have no idea by how much. That is why a growing number of companies now use benchmarking (also called 'best practice benchmarking') to obtain comparative information against other organizations.

> 'Decision-makers in particular should look for signs that they have the support and confidence of senior management.'

The principle behind benchmarking is simple: if you want to improve a particular aspect of your business, find another organization that is extremely good at whatever it is you want to improve and use them as a benchmark for performance improvement.

Benchmarking (which can also be applied to compare different parts of the same organization) is not about cloning the success of others, nor is it about industrial espionage. The goal is both to be able to learn from best practice and to be able to quantify the impact of an initiative or decision.

For example, a manufacturing company which is concerned about delivery times might gather information about the performance of its delivery fleet by benchmarking against a specialist freight carrier. In this way it knows how good it has to be to match an organization that excels in that activity. Also, because the organizations are not in direct competition, it will usually be easier to gain information about how the benchmarked company runs its operations.

Benchmarking can also pave the way for other opportunities. If by benchmarking against a specialist, the manufacturer discovers that its own delivery performance cannot be sufficiently improved, benchmarking can provide valuable information about the advantages of outsourcing that activity.

COPING WITH INFORMATION OVERLOAD

The biggest problem facing decision-makers today is not a lack of information, but the opposite: too much information. Consider the following claims:

- A weekday edition of *The Times* now contains more information than the average person was likely to come across in their entire lifetime during the 17th century.

- More information has been produced in the last 30 years than in the previous 5,000 (with about 1,000 new books published around the world each day).

- The total quantity of all printed material is doubling every five years – and accelerating.

- In the next few years, the digital revolution, still in its infancy at present, is likely to have a huge impact.

No wonder, then, that we are all swimming – or drowning – in information. Psychologist Dr David Lewis, says:

'Having too much information can be as dangerous as having too little. Among other problems, it can lead to a paralysis of analysis, making it harder to find the right solutions or make the best decisions.'[5]

The information glut

Recent research confirms that information overload is now a major problem for many managers. A study published by Reuters in November 1996, for example, claims that an excess of data is strangling business and causing employees to suffer mental anguish and physical ill health. The problem is exacerbated by inadequate IT training and the failure of many organizations to introduce policies and procedures for managing information.

The study, which involved an independent survey of over 1,200 managers around the world,[6] reported that one in four respondents said their health suffered as a result of the volume of information they now handle (although half agreed they needed high levels of information to perform their job effectively). Some 48 per cent also predicted that the Internet would aggravate the problem further in the next two years.

The effects of the information glut, the report suggests, are procrastination and time wasting, leading to the delaying of important decisions, distraction from main job responsibilities, tension between colleagues and loss of job satisfaction. Many of those surveyed also reported that information overload caused high levels of stress resulting in illness and the breakdown of personal relationships.

Clearly, these are worrying findings. But why should information suddenly present such a problem?

According to Paul Waddington, marketing manager at Reuters Business Information, there are two main factors. One, he says, is the huge increase in the volume of information emanating both from within the organization and outside – from customers, suppliers and other sources including the media. At the same time there has been an explosion of enabling technology which people are struggling to understand. As a result information is crashing in on us from all sides.

'There used to be just internal memos and meetings. Now there is e-mail, the Internet and a host of other tools to deal with. In the past people were able to develop ways of filtering information, but now there is such a flood that they can't do that any more.'

Moreover, what few organizations have recognized, he says, is the scale of the change taking place.

'It's partly a function of increasing competition and the lingering effects of downsizing and redundancies which make people feel they are under pressure to make the right decisions. Often, they have so much information that they don't know what to do with it. At the same time they wonder whether their competitors have better or more up-to-date information.'

111

Flaming

A number of managers have reported deliberate sabotage by others in the organization who set out to flame them with unnecessary information which prevents them getting on with their jobs. Typically this will take the form of a deluge of e-mail messages which have little or no value to the organization but which clog up the information channels and waste the time of those who try to read them and reply.

As Dr Lewis notes:

> *'We have certainly come across reports of flame walls created around individuals, where someone is deliberately singled out and flamed with information from all sides – using e-mail for example – just to make their life difficult.'*

Information gatekeepers

In many organizations, the problem of information overload has been compounded by confusion over which function – human resources (HR), public relations (PR) or information technology (IT) – should have the primary responsibility for information management. As a result, many organizations resemble an information war zone where decision-makers face a constant barrage of new and often unhelpful messages.

Comments Dr Lewis:

> *'Many companies are still in the dark ages when it comes to managing the flow of information, trying to communicate everything to everyone. Sometimes a manager will copy a memo to 2,000 people just to show his seniority.'*

Findings from another recent survey published by *Business Intelligence*[7] suggest that the HR function should be taking the lead. The survey, which looked at the strategic management of internal communications, found that HR was seen as the natural gatekeeper of internal communication in 35 per cent of organizations, compared to just 25 per cent who felt that information management was an issue for the PR department.

The recognition that information overload is a potential threat to the well-being of employees adds weight to that finding. Dr Lewis agrees, although he believes the best approach is a cross-functional one:

> *'I think it is an HR issue because it's a human problem, but one that should be tackled in conjunction with other functions including IT.*
>
> *'Really, it's about the interface between the human brain and technology. Information is not knowledge until it has been*

*processed by the human mind. A definition of knowledge is infor-
mation which reduces uncertainty. But too much information
actually increases uncertainty and is very stressful.'*

Alleviating the problem

Given that information overload is fast becoming one of the most per-
nicious time bandits of all, what steps can managers take to alleviate
the problem?

According to Paul Waddington at Reuters, companies need to focus
on effective information-sharing technology, rather than the indiscrimi-
nate approach many have taken so far, and create formal policies and
procedures for information management. Written standards for e-mail
for example, he says, could drastically reduce the problem of junk e-
mail by providing clear guidelines about the sorts of information that
should be circulated and to whom.

*'At present it's not unusual for some managers to receive 60 e-mail
messages a day. Rather than them deciding which they should
respond to and which to ignore, it makes sense to look at how
many of those 60 should have been sent in the first place.'*

DEVELOPING GOOD INFORMATION HABITS

For individual managers, the best protection against information overload is to find more effective ways to manage data. The need for better
information habits is more than just a sensible tactic for decision-
making, it is essential to avoid drowning in the huge quantities of data
that managers have to deal with.

Dr Lewis also sees a pressing need for new sorts of training.

*'On a personal level, people need skills for handling information. Most
people have very bad reading habits, dating back to when they learned
to read out loud at school. They still translate printed symbols into a
voice in their head – sometimes you can even see their lips moving.
That's a major block on their ability to process information. What they
need now is to learn to read in a completely different way; to ask the
data a question, then skim down until they find the answer.'*

Better writing habits would help, too, he says.

*'A lot of senior executives could learn from working as journalists.
It's much easier to write in a complex way than it is to write simply.'*

113

Decision-makers in particular could gain greatly from developing some of the habits explained earlier. They include learning to:

- ask the right questions to narrow down the data required for a decision (fly fishing rather than trawling)
- interrogating the source
- interrogating the data itself to extract the useful nuggets
- testing for bias.

In part, however, the solution relies on organizations streamlining their communication channels so that information is communicated to the people who really need it in the most effective way.

Some specialist internal communications consultancies provide assistance for companies ready to grasp the nettle. The ITEM Group, for example, has recently introduced a new service which involves working with clients to identify best practice in this area. Says David James, a consultant with ITEM:

> 'A lot of companies have introduced electronic communication systems thinking they are a solution to internal communications only to find that if they aren't properly managed they can aggravate the problem. We help clients to integrate systems such as intranets and e-mail with the more traditional forms of communication.'

For example, some companies have decided that e-mail should be used only to communicate operational matters. They provide templates and training to help managers become effective message makers, with a format which clearly identifies the action to be taken. Some of the major supermarket chains are also developing guidelines which cover all forms of communication right down to the appropriate use of store tannoy systems.

DESKTOP DEMOCRATIZATION

According to a number of experts the availability of IT is leading to 'desktop democratization', as more and more people are able to use e-mail and other technology to communicate freely across the organization.

As James explains:

> 'So-called desktop democratization means that everyone has become a message maker and a message sender, which wasn't the case before. It requires a new approach.'

At a strategic level, James says, message segmentation – which involves a clear understanding of the informational needs of different audiences; and content management – ensuring that time isn't wasted dealing with unnecessary information – can help.

Other simple steps include:

- training in separating primary information (that which is essential to the task or decision in hand) from secondary information, which, no matter how interesting, is irrelevant to the specific situation

- more effective pre-analysis filtering of information so that managers receive only what they need to know in order to do their work efficiently

- improved communications – and presentation – skills to cut out needless information and signpost where to find useful information

- clear guidelines on the proper use of different information channels, including e-mail and other IT tools

- templates for regular reports and updates which create a consistent reporting format

- better training in the use of IT tools

- training in prioritizing and information interrogation.

More extreme measures might include:

- managers keeping records of time-wasting e-mail messages

- information audits

- disciplinary procedures for dealing with deliberate sabotage by 'flaming'.

Information stress

Information overload causes stress in a number of ways. There is:

- fear that a failure to understand crucial information will cause us to make costly mistakes

- fear of being overwhelmed by the sheer volume of information that must be mastered to stay on top of our jobs

- fear caused by not knowing whether crucial information exists, or how to check

- 'frustration stress', caused when we know that information exists but don't know how to access it.

▶

▶

Underlying and intensifying information stress are time pressures. The more we have to read and understand, the greater the demands on the hours available. Compelled to choose among a series of options in the face of vast amounts of potentially vital information and against the clock, we move into a state of excessive stress – a hyperaroused psychological condition. The inevitable outcome is impaired decision-making and flawed conclusions.

The business and human cost of information overload

The cost to business

According to the Reuters survey:

- 38 per cent of managers waste substantial amounts of time trying to locate the right information

- 84 per cent of managers feel compelled to collect information just to stay competitive

- 43 per cent think that important decisions are delayed and the ability to make decisions affected as a result of having too much information

- 47 per cent say collection of information for decision-making distracts them from their main job responsibilities

- 44 per cent believe the cost of collecting information exceeds its value to the business.

The human cost

Of the managers reporting information overload:

- two out of three said that stress caused by information overload leads to tension with work colleagues and loss of job satisfaction

- one-third said they suffer ill health as a direct consequence of the quantity of information they have to deal with (the figure rises to 43 per cent among senior managers)

- 49 per cent of all managers regularly work late or take work home with them as a result of having too much information

- 62 per cent say their personal relationships suffer.

Information push or information pull?

Many of these issues come down to finding the best way to provide managers with access to information. In this regard, the new technology, which is currently part of the problem, could also offer the solution.

The problem with e-mail, many people believe, is that it is an information push technology. Messages – some of them containing important information and others little more than junk mail – are pushed out from the source to individuals sitting at their terminals. As such, the manager on the receiving end has no control over the volume or relevance of the information received.

Stories of managers being 'flamed' with messages, or deluged with information, are common. Sometimes it is done with malicious intent. Every time the manager accesses his or her e-mail, they receive literally hundreds of messages which tie up their computer for long periods and prevent them from getting on with their work.

Even where there is no malice intended, managers who try to read and respond to e-mail messages can spend hours every week on irrelevant information. One senior IT manager, asked how useful he found the Internet, groaned: 'I can't keep up with my internal messages – what the hell do I want with the Internet?'

However, recent developments such as intranets – companywide information systems based on worldwide web technology – are based on 'information pull'. Users publish useful data on their own web pages which is then available to anyone else with access to the intranet through their own terminal.

In effect, intranets allow managers to access the information they require, by pulling it down to their terminals. In this way, they can access information from other parts of the business even when the people who own it are not at their desks.

The PR company Burson-Marsteller advises companies setting up intranets. According to Mel Lowe, a consultant in the company's internal communications practice:

> 'The beauty of an intranet is that it changes the dynamics of how information moves around a company from an "information push" process to one of "information pull". Rather than being bombarded with all sorts of information around the organization, employees can pull in the information they need.
>
> 'We're also finding that the more enlightened companies are now talking about knowledge management rather than information management. We do a lot of work helping companies structure web pages using effective signposting and headlining so that the key points can be accessed very quickly.'

117

Reuters, too, has some products which could help. In recent years the company has established a range of on-line information services for corporate users. Its flagship product *Business Briefing* enables managers to dial up and retrieve information according to their own specifications. Users have direct access to current or archive information sources such as newspaper and magazine articles. They can also obtain financial summaries of quoted companies, enabling a manager, for example, to obtain instant background information about a potential client prior to a visit.

PARALYSIS BY ANALYSIS

No matter how good the information a decision-maker gathers, there comes a point where additional information and analysis are not helpful. To some extent the more informed a decision can be the better, but other factors including time pressures, mean that there has to be a cut-off point.

The fact is that after a while additional information subtracts more in confusion and delay than it adds in understanding. Worse still, it leads to procrastination and can result in a phenomenon known as **paralysis by analysis**. This occurs when so much conflicting data is collected that there is no clear answer. The point to bear in mind,

> 'No matter how good the information a decision-maker gathers, there comes a point where additional information and analysis are not helpful.'

however, is that analysis is nothing more than an interpretation of the past. To borrow from a famous quotation: 'The past is a foreign country.' And so is the future.

Enough's enough

As this heading suggests, there comes a point with gathering information where enough is enough. Just where to draw the line requires judgement, but clearly the size and significance of the decision for the organization is an important factor – the decision about which photocopier to buy or rent is less critical than deciding the long-term strategy of the company. The latter justifies the collection of large quantities of data about the market, the former probably no more than three or four quotes. But in the end, it comes down to good decision-making habits.

Gathering and processing information is just one part of the decision. What is also required is the space and time to think. That's why when it comes to collecting data, effective decision-makers know that 'enough's enough'.

References

1. Dawson, Roger, *Make the Right Decision Every Time*, Nicholas Brealey, 1994.

2. Clutterbuck, David, and Goldsmith, Walter, *The Winning Streak Mark II*, Orion, 1997.

3. Van Gunsteren, Lex, *FT Handbook of Management*, Pitman, 1995.

4. Clutterbuck, David, Clark, Graham, and Aronistead, Colin, *Inspired Customer Service*, Kogan Page, 1993.

5. Dearlove, Des, 'Junk Information', *Human Resources*, Issue 29, March/April 1997.

6. Reuters, *Information Overload*, 1996.

7. *Is Anyone Listening*, Business Intelligence, 1995.

Decision-making structures

'The man who is denied the opportunity of taking decisions of importance begins to regard as important the decisions he is allowed to take.'
C NORTHCOTE PARKINSON,
management writer and academic

'Decisions have to be made where the knowledge is. I believe professionals have rights within the organization. I believe they need rights to do their jobs.'
CHARLES HANDY, management writer

'The costs of hierarchical decision-making are now too high to bear. Referring everything up the ladder means decisions get made too slowly for a fast-paced market.'
MICHAEL HAMMER AND JAMES CHAMPY
Re-engineering the Corporation

An important factor affecting decision-making is the structure – or shape – of the organization. In recent years, many companies have moved to flatter management structures, or in some cases new sorts of structures altogether. The logic is twofold: to make the organization more responsive to the marketplace by ensuring decisions are made closer to the customer; and to speed up the decision-making process by shortening reporting lines.

Yet in many cases, restructuring and shorter reporting lines are not mirrored by a corresponding change in the internal culture. So, although the formal structure of the organization may be flat, the culture remains hierarchical. Research – and common sense – suggests that in these circumstances, the culture

> 'An important factor affecting decision-making is the structure – or shape – of the organization.'

will override the formal structure. (Culture is discussed in Chapter 7.)

Here, we consider the formal structures and reporting lines which support or hinder effective decision-making. The traditional organizational models can be grouped as follows:

- the military model of command and control
- functional chimneys
- the multi-divisional structure
- matrix management (multinationals).

More recent innovations are:

- the shamrock organization
- membership communities
- the star
- the boundaryless organization
- the amoeba organization
- the chemical soup organization – project teams
- the virtual organization.

We also consider a number of other related issues, including the effects of:

- flatter management structures
- downsizing

- business process re-engineering
- longer reporting spans

and their impact on:

- delegation
- accountability.

THE MILITARY MODEL

The traditional decision-making structures of companies were based on the military model. In essence, authority was determined by seniority – or rank – within the hierarchy. Decision-making followed the command and control approach, which underpinned traditional corporate structures.

The chief advantage of this sort of structure is that it allows the centre, or senior individuals within the hierarchy, to effectively issue orders which will be followed without question. The idea is that this enables them to determine the direction of strategy, while allowing tactical decisions to be made closer to the action. Because it is a highly disciplined structure, it also allows the chief executive to take control into his own hands and command his troops when the organization is threatened.

The main drawback of this structure, however, is that it relies on the few at the top having a clear sight of what's going on – whether it is in the marketplace or on the field of battle – in order to determine strategy. When they lose touch with what's happening on the ground, the result can be catastrophic.

As the former president of Avis, Robert Townsend, observed: 'The charge of the Light Brigade was ordered by an officer who wasn't there looking down at the territory.'

In management terms, the command and control approach also relies on high levels of discipline to ensure workers do what they are told. In this model, middle managers are akin to sheep dogs, whose primary role is to direct the flock. Moreover, the company is vulnerable if top management does not take decisive action as no one else has the authority to do so.

Highly hierarchical organizations of this kind also tend to suffer from bureaucracy. Decision-making in anything other than a crisis is usually extremely slow and prone to red tape as all decisions have to be referred up the hierarchy to the appropriate level.

Corporate hierarchies

In the corporate world, Henry Ford's production line approach epitomized the military model. Ford based his plants on Taylorism, the idea that work could be broken down into a series of simple tasks which workers carried out without any reference to the work of others.

He relied on a high level of discipline among workers, which was enforced by managers. Higher-than-average wages were seen as a sufficiently strong motivator to persuade workers to accept mindless obedience to the managerial machine. But many employees soon became dispirited by the work they were required to do and when productivity fell were simply replaced by new workers lured by the appeal of high rewards.

To some extent, employee turnover rates at Ford's factories indicate a corporate machine that chewed people up and spat them out again in a short space of time. But Ford was able to keep the cars rolling off the production line because of a plentiful supply of unskilled labour.

Over time, the division of labour approach spawned a series of functional specialisms which gave rise to the predominate corporate structure right through to the 1960s.

FUNCTIONAL CHIMNEYS

As companies grew ever larger and more complex, the increasing requirement for specialists gave rise to a structure best described as a series of functional chimneys or silos. Finance specialists worked in the finance function, marketing specialists in the marketing department and so on In these functional structures, there was a clear demarcation of skills. Similar demarcations among shopfloor workers, which can be seen as a direct legacy of Taylorism, were also institutionalized by trade unions which jealously guarded their patch.

It was only in the 1980s that the union stranglehold on working practices was broken allowing for multi-skilling among workers. However, the traditional demarcation of managers has survived relatively unscathed in many organizations.

Defenders of the functional approach argue that it works. Indeed, companies have been structured along these lines for the greater part of the 20th century. Critics, however, point out that although the system has not failed, it is incredibly inefficient.

In particular, there tends to be little cross-fertilization of ideas between functions. In decision-making terms, it also leads to decisions made in functional vacuums without a proper understanding of the implications for other departments. A marketing manager, for example, decides to launch a new product that if he'd bothered to ask them, R&D or production could have told him won't work.

125

There is also a tendency for functional chimneys to be inward-looking and lose touch with what's going on in the marketplace. The functional specialists can become so caught up in internal politics that they overlook the customers. As a result, this model is now largely out of fashion with management commentators (even though it continues to be widespread among companies).

THE MULTI-DIVISIONAL STRUCTURE

Even though the shortcomings of the functional structure were soon apparent, the solution proved elusive. One of the most influential attempts to create a new sort of structure was that of Alfred P Sloan, who became president of General Motors in 1923, chairman in 1946, and was honorary chairman from 1956 until his death a decade later.[1]

As Sumantra Ghoshal from London Business School notes:

'Sloan created a new organizational form – the multi-divisional form – which became a doctrine of management. Today, it is not ascribed to him, but Sloan was its instigator.'

In effect what Sloan did at GM was to organize the company along federal lines, replacing the bureaucracy-riddled system with a number of divisions or operating businesses. Each of the 30 or so divisions had its own clearly delineated responsibilities. In the marketplace, GM's products – including Chevrolet and Cadillac – competed as separate identities and were managed by different divisions which were given a high level of autonomy by the centre.

This structure allowed GM to overtake Ford. But Sloan's approach relied on a delicate balancing act between centralized decision-making and decentralized decision-making. It also relied on a complex web of committees which over time descended into turf wars and political manoeuvring. By the 1960s, the finance function had emerged as the dominant function and the delicate balance was lost.

Despite GM falling off its pedestal, the multi-divisional structure was emulated by other companies and continued to be a corporate blueprint up until the late 1980s. By the 1990s, however, it became clear to many that it was too cumbersome a structure to provide the flexibility and speed of decision-making required to compete in global markets.

As Jack Welch, chairman of General Electric, observed: 'It was right for the 1970s, a growing handicap in the 1980s and would have been a ticket to the bone-yard in the 1990s.'[2]

That said, it is only now that more flexible, entrepreneurial structures are beginning to emerge.

MATRIX MANAGEMENT

Really a variation on the multi-divisional model, matrix management is an organizational structure which is not based on a simple chain of command, but where individuals report to two (or more) bosses.

This sort of structure was adopted by many multinational companies. As much as anything, matrix management was an attempt to clarify responsibilities and reporting lines in large companies with operations in more than one national market.

Under a typical matrix management system, a marketing manager in, say, Germany reports ultimately to a boss in that country, but also to the head of the marketing function back in the company's home country. The two reporting lines are the two sides to the matrix, which has a geographical and a functional axis.

As a theoretical model, the matrix is a neat solution to the complexity of large companies. However, in reality, power cannot be evenly balanced, and conflicts inevitably arise. When you include additional complexity such as cross-functional reporting lines in project teams or start-up operations, the poor marketing manager can find herself trying to please several different bosses at the same time.

The real question with a matrix structure is, 'Where does the power lie?' Is it with the national manager, or is it with the function head back at HQ? Attempts to resolve these sorts of problems have been largely a case of fudging the decision-making structure to suit the circumstance. Many multinationals continue to operate as matrix management structures simply because they haven't come up with a better model.

Hierarchies under attack

In recent years, the whole notion of hierarchical decision-making has come under attack. In today's fast-moving markets, companies recognize an increasing need to stay close to customers and ensure that day-to-day decisions are made as close to the action as possible.

At the same time, social pressures and the emergence of knowledge workers – who demand greater freedom of action to do their jobs – has led to a backlash against the whole command and control edifice.

▶

▶

> Many commentators also believe that advances in information technology render the old structures obsolete.
>
> 'The hierarchy is under siege because it's increasingly inefficient and many of the most effective workers in our companies are sick of it', notes Harvard Business School's D Quinn Mills.[3]
>
> *'They're tired of the rituals, the lack of real communication, the delays in making decisions and taking action. With new technology diffusing information widely, many feel that the issue isn't who you are in the structure but what you get accomplished.'*
>
> This has led to the emergence of new organizational models such as the shamrock organization and membership communities which have important implications for the decision-making process.

THE SHAMROCK ORGANIZATION

The 'shamrock organization' is a term coined by management writer Charles Handy to describe a type of organizational structure with three parts – or leaves.[4] It is defined as a 'form of organization based around a core of essential executives and workers supported by outside contractors and part-time help'.

This model, or variations of it, are often used to explain the move to outsourcing non-core functions. In Handy's analogy, the first leaf of the shamrock represents the core staff of the organization. These people are likely to be highly trained professionals who make up the senior management.

The second leaf consists of the contractual fringe, either individuals or other organizations, and often consists of people who once worked for the organization but now provide it with services. These individuals operate within the broad framework set down by the core, but have a high level of discretionary decision-making power to complete projects or deliver contracts.

The third leaf includes the flexible labour force. More than simply hired hands, in Handy's model, these workers have to be sufficiently close to the organization to feel a sense of commitment which ensures that their work – although part-time or intermittent – is carried out to a high standard. The decision-making authority of these workers will typically be limited to their own work.

MEMBERSHIP COMMUNITIES

Interestingly, Handy has now taken this model several steps further by suggesting that successful organizations of the future will be what he calls 'membership communities'. His logic is that in order to hold people to an organization which can no longer promise them a job for life, companies have to offer some other form of continuity and sense of belonging. To do this, he suggests, companies have to imbue members with certain rights.

What Handy is advocating in fact is some notion of a federal organization, built on the principle of subsidiarity. This places a large degree of trust in its core professionals and other knowledge workers. As he told Joel Kurtzman in an interview for *Strategy & Business* recently:[5]

'You must leave as much power as low as possible in the organization, as that's where the knowledge and experience are. It seems to me that subsidiarity is at the heart of professionalism. Think for a moment about the doctor in the emergency room of a hospital. The doctor is in charge even though she may be straight out of medical school and her speciality training. The doctor is in total charge in that place at that time because she has the knowledge and the skills. As a consequence all the decisions are hers to make.

'This is how I conceive of the members of the corporation . . . Decisions have to be made where the knowledge is. So I believe professionals have rights within the organization. I believe they need rights to do their jobs.'

Under Handy's membership community model, the centre is kept small and its primary purpose is to be 'in charge of the future'. Only if the organization is severely threatened does decision-making power revert to the centre. This allows the company to react quickly in a crisis. The rest of the time, decision-making is highly decentralized.

In this sense, it is similar to the United States of America, where authority over foreign policy and other issues affecting national security reside in Washington, but the individual states retain much of the power over local decisions. At times of great threat to the survival of the USA, however, power flows to the executive arm, so that the president has complete authority over the armed forces as commander in chief. The same, Handy suggests, should happen with the new-style company.

New structures

Handy's ground-breaking work has also prompted other new models. According to management author David Clutterbuck, the new structures emerging are many and varied, but tend to fall into one or other of the following categories:[6]

- the star
- the boundaryless organization
- the amoeba organization
- the chemical soup organization – project teams.

THE STAR

Star organizations are built around a small number of large customers. Everything they do mirrors a customer need. They may operate from the customer's premises and may even have absorbed some of the customer's former staff. The majority of people in the organization are concerned with delivery and they are supported by a relatively small core of experts and administrative staff. The pace of organizational change and decision-making is partially or wholly dictated by that of the customer, although part of the customer expectation may be that the star organization stimulates the cultural and technical innovation that its own people cannot. Typical star organizations would be IT contractors such as Perot Systems or the FI Group.

Routine decisions are made by staff on the ground, who report important changes back to the centre for the purposes of making strategic decisions.

THE BOUNDARYLESS ORGANIZATION

Boundaryless organizations have abandoned the attempt to maintain the distinction between their operations and those of their suppliers and customers. They operate through networks of expert sub-contractors, mostly smaller businesses than themselves or self-employed freelancers. They enter into joint ventures with customers and freely second their own staff to customers' organizations. They retain their identity by remaining within a clearly defined market niche and venturing outside that niche only in partnerships with other similar organizations. Typical boundaryless organizations are specialist management consultancies. Their culture is pragmatic, strongly individualistic and heavily reliant on relationships.

They have an extremely high discretionary decision-making approach, with individuals expected to solve problems either on their own or by accessing expertise elsewhere in the organization through networking.

THE AMOEBA ORGANIZATION

Amoebas grow fast and split instinctively when they feel they are beginning to lose touch with their customers. They also have strong instincts of customer-orientation and innovation. People in these organizations are motivated by the chance to run their own show – empowerment is built into the structures and systems. Amoebas may also be characterized by disorganized systems, especially around the 'soft' issues of management – they rarely stand still for long enough to put these in order. Typical amoeba organizations might be young, entrepreneurial high-technology companies.

Decision-making in amoebas may appear chaotic, but is usually extremely fast and effective as long as the lines of accountability do not become strained. Amoebas can get bogged down when they grow too large without splitting, and lines of authority become blurred. They rely on the entrepreneurial instincts of their managers.

THE CHEMICAL SOUP ORGANIZATION

The chemical soup organization differs from the boundaryless organization in that while the latter has a clear framework of fixed structures and reporting lines, in which people find their own freedom to operate, the chemical soup organization often appears to have no fixed structures at all. The main driving force, outside of the senior management vision, is a motley collection of ever-changing project teams. No job or task is permanent; changing circumstances arising from changing customer needs, market opportunity or some internal drive for efficiency dictate that teams and their members come and go constantly and often at short notice. Working in a chemical soup organization is unsettling, challenging, sometimes frustrating (people often feel that nothing ever gets finished), but the outputs and speed of decisions often generate rapid growth and high returns for both the companies and the people who work for them.

Chemical soup companies are often relatively large organizations, going through rapid growth or cultural transformation. Decision-making is the result of chemical reactions taking place within the organization and happens on an *ad hoc* basis, with individuals behaving as followers and leaders, often within the same working day, as they switch between different roles.

THE VIRTUAL ORGANIZATION

Perhaps the most radical structural model of all is the virtual organization, which taken to the extreme involves no structure at all.

Much beloved of management theorists, the notion of the virtual organization has more than one interpretation. To some people, it refers simply to the ability of companies to use IT to allow people in different locations, and even on different continents, to work together effectively.

Using IT, it is argued, employees no longer need to come into the office at all and can work remotely from their homes or different offices anywhere around the globe, plugging into a virtual community that is made possible by technology.

In this way, companies can dismantle their cumbersome headquarters buildings, the costly bricks and mortar of the conventional business. Employees can work at home or in satellite offices when required. Linked by networks of computers, communicating by e-mail and modems, workers are freed from the burdens of commuting and the daily grind of office work. With no expensive tower blocks to support, organizations can make massive savings.

> 'Perhaps the most radical structural model of all is the virtual organization . . .'

Others regard this as simply the beginning. A number of companies have found that virtual working allows the traditional structure of the organization to be discarded altogether. They advocate an organizational model which can bring together individuals or companies to work on a single project, where the virtual organization or team exists only for as long as it is required to complete the project and is then disbanded.

Virtual teams: here today, gone tomorrow

One way to think of this is in terms of the cast of a film or play who come together to form a team for as long as the show is in production and then go their separate ways. Specialists can also belong to several virtual organizations simultaneously, ensuring that their skills are used in an optimal way.

What all the variations of the virtual organization have in common is that they start from the premise that IT now enables individuals in different locations to work together unhindered by geographical separation. Their ability to communicate and share information also means that the patterns of decision-making are fundamentally altered, with no necessity for co-ordination from the centre.

If we think of individual workers as dots on the organizational map, then one justification for traditional structures was to provide a means to direct their efforts. But as soon as you can connect each dot – or computer terminal – to any other the need for a formal structure disappears.

If we go a step further and think of those dots as light bulbs connected with the power of communication, then, theoretically at least, a virtual organization can instantly light up any pattern or configuration of skills required, and can switch it off just as quickly.

CASE STUDY: VERIFONE

At VeriFone – a California-based company which dominates the US credit card authorization market – the virtual concept has been taken further than most. VeriFone's CEO Hatim Tyabji explained to management writer Tom Peters:[7]

> 'VeriFone's organizational model is the blueberry pancake: independent units (blueberries) held together by a unifying medium (batter).'

The company is highly decentralized and claims to have no headquarters. Instead, each part – or blueberry – is expected to generate its own ideas and strategies and ultimately to make its own decisions.

In the blueberry pancake model, instant communication via e-mail is an essential ingredient. Employees get a laptop before they get a desk and internal paper mail is banned. Mr Tyabji says:

> 'The company is run 100 per cent electronically. There is no paper. E-mail is the lifeblood of this company. It is direct communication, totally unfiltered. At first, some people don't think they can handle 75 e-mail messages a day, but just as you get junk mail, you get junk e-mail. It's a matter of learning to separate the important from the trivial.'

Eliminating paper, he says, creates a 'culture of urgency' which has allowed him as chief executive to break free of the manacles that keep other senior managers chained to their desks. It means he can

▶

play a more active role in the business, spending between 80 and 90 per cent of his time on the road.

'It would be impossible for me to run a traditional company and travel as much as I do. All those reports and memos would pile up until I got back. Then I'd have to read them and respond. Instead of all that, wherever I am in the world, I sit down at my laptop and instantly respond. When I go back to my office, the only thing on the desk is p-mail – physical mail – usually magazines.'

Staff at VeriFone know, too, that anyone in the company – no matter how junior – is free to e-mail Tyabji direct wherever he is.

'I tell people that I don't mind being overrun with e-mail. In fact, I personally respond to every piece of e-mail within 24 hours.'

For most companies, true virtual working is still some way off. But the trend towards flatter management structures is clear.

FLATTER MANAGEMENT STRUCTURES

Whatever the models, in the business world of the 1990s, fat is out and flat is in. Much of the restructuring over recent years has involved cutting out layers of middle management 'fat' to create 'lean' management structures. The logic for this is that hierarchy breeds bureaucracy; removing it liberates people to make their own decisions, which in turn improves efficiency.

That much of the 'de-layering' also occurred during the recession of the early 1990s is no coincidence, of course. In many companies the move to flatter structures has been driven by the need to cut costs by making redundancies among their management populations.

A number of management theories and ideas have also had a major influence on the move to flatter structures and the way companies think about decision-making.

DOWNSIZING

The term 'downsizing' was coined by the American management academic Stephen Roach. He advocated a wholesale reduction in staffing levels as the key to greater efficiency. Originally intended as the antidote to the growing bureaucracy within large American organizations, down-sizing became a flag of convenience for many organizations looking to reduce costs by cutting headcount.

In many cases, downsizing and de-layering were pursued with such vigour and disregard for the human cost, that its victims and survivors alike came to regard it as little more than a cynical exercise.

Confronted by the unpalatable face of capitalism, even Roach himself has since recanted, claiming that many companies took downsizing too far and used it for the wrong purposes.

BUSINESS PROCESS RE-ENGINEERING (BPR)

Allied to the downsizing trend is another management cure-all: business process re-engineering (BPR). BPR has been one of the most significant influences on management thinking in the past few years.

As described in *The Business Magazine*, BPR 'involves fundamentally rethinking and redesigning the processes, which we often take for granted, in order to achieve dramatic improvements in business performance.' It requires managers to map and analyze core processes in detail, from beginning (for example, R&D) to end (e.g., final delivery to the customer). Departmental barriers are ignored in the exercise – it is the process that counts. The idea is to create a much simpler process, with fewer layers of management and a radically different organizational structure.

Re-engineering the Corporation – the book that started the ball rolling – was published in the UK in 1993. In it, its American authors Michael Hammer and James Champy set out what they described as a 'manifesto for business revolution'.[8]

Far from revolutionary, however, many commentators have observed that re-engineering was simply a logical next step following on from scientific management (Taylorism), industrial engineering, and business process improvement (TQM). What re-engineering really had going for it was that it fitted the needs of companies looking for a reason to continue the attack on bureaucracy and complacency, and with them the traditional hierarchical decision-making structures.

In essence, the message of BPR was that organizations needed to identify their key processes and 're-engineer' them to make them as efficient as possible. To some extent, then, BPR was the sword to cut the Gordian knot of bureaucracy that had become institutionalized in many companies. In particular, it advocated that peripheral processes and by implication peripheral employees should be stripped away.

As with TQM before it, a thriving consultancy business has also grown fat on advising companies about how to implement BPR.

Re-engineering management

The BPR revolution was all about re-engineering processes within organizations. But to date it has left management processes largely untouched. Hence the title of Champy's sequel *Re-engineering Management*.

> '*It is now time to re-engineer the manager. Senior managers have been re-engineering business processes with a passion, tearing down corporate structures that no longer support the organization. Yet the practice of management has largely escaped demolition. If their jobs and styles are left largely intact, managers will eventually undermine the very structure of their rebuilt enterprises.*'

As one of the key management processes is that of decision-making, re-engineering may yet have a radical influence on the way that decisions are made in future.

Letting people run their own show

Flatter management structures mean fewer rungs on the corporate ladder, which in turn means fewer opportunities for promotion. Whatever the logic driving de-layering, what is clear from a number of studies is that faced with fewer opportunities for promotion, managers see greater autonomy – or decision-making power – as an alternative source of reward.

The *Ashridge Management Index*, an annual survey carried out by Ashridge School of Management, is a barometer of managers' attitudes and lifestyles based on a survey of 500 middle and senior managers.[9]

When asked what really motivates them, 61 per cent of respondents in the 1996 survey put challenging and interesting work first. Other high-scoring motivators included 'letting people run their own show' and 'seeing the impact of decisions on the business'. These factors – along with high basic salary (35 per cent) – came top of the motivation league table. Dr Laurence Handy, director of the Ashridge Management Research Group says:

> '*Our results suggest that many managers have now adjusted to the restructuring that has taken place. What they want now is the right sort of support from senior management so that they can get on with their jobs without someone breathing down their necks the whole time.*'

LONGER REPORTING SPANS

The move to flatter management structures has two inevitable consequences. It means that reporting lines are becoming shorter – with fewer layers of management separating those in the boardroom from those on the shopfloor. It also means that spans of control are greater, with managers having direct responsibility for a larger number of employees. These two factors place a greater emphasis on delegation.

Elliott Jacques, the path-breaking Canadian psychologist who was a founder of the Tavistock Institute of Human Relations in London, conducted a series of studies on the factory floor of the Glacier Metal Company between 1948 and 1965.

He is most famous for having developed a theory of the value of work based on the *time span of discretion,* which basically said that different levels of management should be based on how long it was before their decisions could be checked, and that people should be paid accordingly.

Jacques was well ahead of his time in many respects. He was one of the first to stress that organization charts do not tell the true story of who reports to whom, and that wise executives knew who their real managers and subordinates were, and acted accordingly. He was also one of the first to realize the importance of changing company culture and of employees feeling that the firm was run fairly.

Others believe that de-layering has altered the reporting spans in many organizations without providing sufficient support for managers who have to adapt to the new way of operating. Dr Barrie Brown, a consultant psychologist and assistant director of studies at Ashridge Management College says:

> *'The traditional view was that the optimal span for reporting lines was seven. Older managers – people aged 40 and over – were taught that directing the work of more than seven people makes it very difficult to remain in control. But some companies now have reporting spans of up to 150 people.'*

As Dr Brown points out, flatter management structures make delegation of some decisions vital.

> *'If you double the number of people a manager is overseeing, then unless the manager delegates authority his workload will automatically double too.'*

THE CHANGING ART OF DELEGATION

One of the most obvious effects of downsizing, BPR and de-layering is that there are fewer middle managers in many organizations than was formerly the case. What this means, observes Jean-Louis Barsoux, a senior research fellow at INSEAD, is that the demands on those who remain are increasing.[10]

Unless they learn to delegate more, he says, managers risk becoming so swamped in work that they will cease to be effective. But fear about their own job security and performance makes many unwilling to trust their work to subordinates.

As Barsoux points out:

> 'Trusting other people to do things as well as you would is a real problem for some people. In many organizations, the culture encourages people to take complete control and to see that as valuable – as the right way to behave.'

The problem, it seems, is that companies want it both ways. Increases in the number of staff that managers oversee are frequently accompanied by making them more accountable for results. This makes some managers reluctant to delegate authority to make decisions.

The problem for managers is learning to let go of power during a time of major change when they feel most inclined to clutch to their authority. The other side of the delegation equation is empowerment – enabling people lower down the organization to accept that they are jointly responsible for achieving objectives.

Avoiding burn-out

To avoid burn-out, managers must learn to cope with their dependence on other people. Yet most will have been promoted to their current positions because they showed themselves to be more dynamic or more effective decision-makers than their colleagues. They are often justified in thinking they can do a better job than those reporting to them. But increasingly, their role is that of coaching others to get things done rather than carrying out tasks themselves.

So how should they react? According to Barsoux, the new management structures mean that the 'Hamlet model of delegation' – to delegate or not to delegate? – once advocated by management textbooks is all but redundant. To delegate or not to delegate is no longer the question; the issue now is *what* to delegate, to *whom*, *when* and *how*?

Rather, managers need to clear the decks, he says, by asking them-selves the question, 'What can't I delegate?' The list will rarely stretch much beyond performance reviews and perhaps budgets. There are few meetings, for example, to which they could not send a deputy; or tasks which an experienced subordinate could not handle.

Managers should then think clearly about what responsibilities they wish to retain. These should be the areas they see as critical; those issues on which a foul-up would jeopardize the future of the company, under-mine the credibility of the department, or reflect badly on them and their judgement.

Three strands of delegation

Barsoux suggests that there are three strands to effective delegation:

- knowing what to delegate
- developing trust in subordinates
- timing.

There is a tendency in drawing up this mental list to let personal prefer-ences intrude, he notes. It is quite natural for managers to try to hang on to the aspects of the job they like doing. But while retaining 'a little of what you fancy' is no doubt important to managerial well-being, too many managers abuse their prerogative by hoarding the interesting work and hiving off the rest. As Peter Webber, managing director of the Andrews Sykes group observes:

> *'In most cases where I have to have a word with one of my man-agers, it's not that they're doing a bad job – it's just that they're doing the wrong job.'*

Once they have established what should be delegated, managers have then to consider the quality of their people. In order to give trust – essential if authority is to be shared – the manager must have confidence in the subordinate it is invested in. This is more difficult with new or unknown subordinates. But a lack of confidence in others often conceals an unwillingness to delegate authority. Properly managed and supported with the necessary training, delegating decisions as well as tasks is an excellent way to develop subordinates.

This introduces the third strand of delegation, namely *timing*. Subordi-nates will be at different stages of their development. The manager has to take care to nurture their capacity for taking on responsibility by investing the right level of authority. Depending on the person and the task in question, a manager may opt for a cursory discussion about the intended approach, or require written progress reports right through to completion.

Thus, there is an on-going process of building confidence and relaxing control. To develop subordinates, the manager must decide when they are ripe to take on more responsibility. And having increased it, the manager must be prepared to sit back and wait – for there can be no trust unless control is also relinquished. To interfere would be to violate the trust. Yet the manager must remain sensitive to the subordinate's needs – and look for signs that hand-holding, advice or encouragement may be required.

Finally, there is the issue of how to delegate. Delegation is not a matter of dumping work on subordinates. Peter Webber says:

'When you delegate, you have to put in the work upfront. You have to learn to get others to do what you want, but of their own volition. They will want a chance to discuss the issue, if only to impress on you what a complex job it is, and to let you express confidence in them.'

As Barsoux concludes:

'The key to delegation, then, is that elusive managerial commodity, judgement. Essentially it is about relinquishing authority for the right things, to the right people, in the right way, at the right time. The hardest lessons of delegation are having faith in your own judgement, and putting faith in other people.'

If the new decision-making structures are to work in the future, however, acquiring that confidence will be essential.

The next step from delegation is empowerment. Empowerment is the vital cultural complement to the new flatter management structures. As such, it is discussed in the next chapter.

Meddlers and muddlers

The other side of delegating is meddling. The chief executive at one medium-sized company was famous within the company's culture for the amount of time he spent changing light bulbs and doing other odd jobs around the office. The fact was that because he had started the company and built it up from nothing, he was used to turning his hand to any task. As the business grew, however, he continued to expend valuable senior management time on trivial tasks. Although the company continues to thrive today, that time might have been better spent on 'bigger issues'.

He is not alone. The same pattern is repeated many times in companies up and down the country. Managers are promoted to bigger jobs but seem hell-bent on rolling up their sleeves at the slightest excuse to get their hands dirty. Often, they manufacture situations.

There is, of course, a valid reason for senior managers to do this on occasions. The most accomplished leaders recognize that time spent 'mucking in' has a big impact on morale and motivation. But managers who persist in interfering do so for no other reason than poor management. To be fair, this is often not entirely their own fault.

Many technically able people are promoted into management jobs that they don't really want. For some reason, there is a tendency in Western organizations in particular to promote someone simply because they are good at their current job regardless of whether they want to move.

As a result, many managers are plucked from the job they love (and are extremely effective in), and put into a role they hate and where their talents are wasted or simply inappropriate. It is no wonder, then, that they hanker to get back to what they are really good at.

> 'If a manager is spending too much time on decisions that should be made by someone else, it also probably means that bigger decisions that belong to their own role are being neglected.'

Unfortunately, however, their actions create other problems which detract from the organization's effectiveness. For one thing, the manager is getting involved in operational decisions that are no longer his to make. If it persists, this will have a negative effect on those below.

At best, it will be seen as meddling. At worst, it will undermine the authority of the new incumbent, and prevent him or her from developing in the role. If allowed to continue indefinitely it may even result in a talented younger manager seeking employment elsewhere.

If a manager is spending too much time on decisions that should be made by someone else, it also probably means that bigger decisions that belong to their own role are being neglected.

As Richard Phillips from Ashridge Management College observes:

> *'Managers should remember that when they perform a task which someone else could do, they prevent themselves from doing a task which only they can do.'*

ACCOUNTABILITY

Whatever the formal structure of the organization, in decision-making terms it serves one important purpose. That is to determine where within the organization accountability should lie.

Faced with possibly the cruellest decision in the history of mankind, whether to use the atomic bomb, President Harry Truman was in no doubt that '*the buck stops here*'.

This is important. But the ability of an organization to change its decision-making practice depends on the culture of the organization – something we will consider in the next chapter.

References

1. Sloan, A P, *My Years with General Motors*, Doubleday, New York, 1963.

2. Crainer, Stuart, *Key Management Ideas*, Pitman, 1996.

3. Mills, D Q, *The Rebirth of the Corporations*, John Wiley, 1991.

4. Handy, C, *The Age of Unreason*, Century Business Books, London, 1989.

5. Kurtzman, Joel, 'An interview with Charles Handy', *Strategy & Business*, Issues 1–3, 1995–1996.

6. Clutterbuck, David, and Dearlove, Des, 'The Charity as a Business', *Directory of Social Change*, 1996.

7. Peters, Tom, *The Tom Peters Seminar: Crazy times call for crazy organizations*, Vintage Books, Random House, New York, 1994.

8. Hammer, M, and Champy, J, *Re-engineering the Corporation*, Harper Business, New York, 1993.

9. *Ashridge Management Index*, 1996, Ashridge Management Research Group, Ashridge School of Management.

10. Barsoux, Jean-Louis, unpublished article, 'The changing art of delegation'.

Decision-making cultures

'My role is that of a catalyst. I try to create an environment in which others make decisions. Success means not making them myself.'
RICARDO SEMLER, author of *Maverick*

'In most organizations it's the informal structure that actually makes things happen regardless of the official mangement structure.'
JOHN TOWERS,
former chief executive of Rover Cars

'It's hard to find a decision-maker these days. So it's best to make a decision on your own, right or wrong. Do something. Make things happen. It's inaction that kills.'
TOM PETERS, management writer

Whatever the formal structure of an organization, the way in which decisions are made will depend on the internal culture – the informal structure and style – of the company. As such, an understanding of the way that the culture operates, its biases, and intolerances, is also vital to allow decision-makers to function effectively.

As business becomes ever more international in scope, requiring managers to apply their skills across borders, national cultural differences, too, can have important effects on the decision-making process. Managers who have been involved in joint ventures or negotiating deals with their counterparts from other national cultures will know only too well the frustrations that can arise from cultural clashes and misunderstandings.

In other cases, companies have tried to impose their corporate cultures on employees from other national cultures, or have gone into joint ventures with companies with very different cultures. What managers in these companies are finding is that an understanding of cultural differences is essential to plug into the decision-making process.

In this chapter we consider these two different strands of culture:

1. **Internal cultures, including:**

   - Ed Schein's three levels of culture
   - empowerment
   - managers as facilitators
   - learning organizations
   - blame cultures and gain cultures
   - managing mistakes
   - groupthink
   - politics and personalities

> '... an understanding of cultural differences is essential to plug into the decision-making process.'

2. **National cultures, including:**

   - the Japanese model of decision-making
   - living with cultural diversity and Trompenaar's four cultural models: family, Eiffel Tower, guided missile and incubator
   - culture clashes
   - Brake's culture prism.

We begin with internal cultures.

145

1. INTERNAL CULTURES

Organizations are built around cultural assumptions as much as they are around structures. Indeed, its culture is so fundamental to the way a company operates that to leave it out of the decision-making equation is at best short-sighted and at worst suicidal. Yet a great many companies ignore culture when they attempt to alter the decision-making environment.

Ed Schein's three levels of culture

Professor Ed Schein of MIT's Sloan School of Management in America provides one of the best-known and most useful models of culture.[1] According to Schein, an organization's culture is made up of lessons that the organization has learnt over the course of its history. Culture, then, he says, is the set of basic assumptions which have worked well enough in the past to be considered 'valid'. Typically there will be three distinct levels:

- behaviour (artefactual level)
- values and principles
- underlying assumptions.

At the **behavioural or artefactual level** are the visible aspects of the organization's culture – its physical layout, office landscape, dress codes, slogans, noise levels and emotional climate. This is the level most apparent to outsiders. These 'artefacts' clearly say something important about the organization, but it is difficult to know precisely what they signify unless you are a participant in the culture.

If you ask managers and employees about their visible behaviour patterns you can begin to build up a picture of the second level of culture – the **values and principles** on which the observed behaviour is based.

So, if we contrast the culture of a bank with that of an advertising agency: the bank's culture may reflect a belief that success depends on rigid financial controls, conservatism and a respect for the management hierarchy. Conversely, the culture of the advertising agency may be based on a belief that success depends on individuals thinking for themselves. In this case, there will be less respect for authority and a livelier exchange of views. In both organizations, the culture will be supported by stories of past events that are part of the organization's folklore and which support its values.

At the third level, is the essence of the culture – **the underlying assumptions** from which both the behaviour and the values are derived. In the bank, for example, this may be an implicit assumption that customers expect the management of their money to be undertaken in a highly ordered and serious manner. The advertising agency, on the other hand, may assume its customers demand a challenging and creative environment that constantly questions sacred cows.

What has not been fully grasped by many organizations yet is that simply changing the decision-making structure will not alter the process by which decisions are made unless the change is accompanied by a change in the culture. In other words, it's not enough to simply tell people in a previously hierarchical organization that they are empowered to make decisions if the culture remains rooted in the old command and control mind-set.

Moreover, if they see that the message is actually contradicted by the finance function – which is saying there is no additional money for training or for making discretionary decisions to satisfy customers, then they will quickly decide that no real change has taken place.

If their own experience tells them, too, that management doesn't mean what it is saying – for example, their boss refuses to delegate decision-making powers – then they will continue to pass decisions up. Which brings us quite neatly to empowerment.

Empowerment

'Empowerment' is one of the most overused (and misused) words to enter the business lexicon in recent years. As the word suggests, empowerment is all about empowering people – providing them with power. Logically, that means the power to make decisions.

In most companies, however, empowerment best describes the aspiration of companies to cascade decision-making power down the organization, so that the people performing tasks have greater control over the way they are performed. Worthy as that aspiration may be, often it fails to translate into practice.

Where empowerment began

The origins of the empowerment movement among Western companies can be traced back to the late 1970s.

In 1979, at the time when Japanese companies and management techniques were wiping the floor with the competition, Konosuke Matsushita of Matsushita Corporation, gave a presentation to a group of American and European managers on a visit to Japan. Describing the commercial battle ahead, he quietly explained:

▶

147

▶

> 'We are going to win and the industrial West is going to lose. There's nothing you can do about it, because the reasons for your failure are within yourselves. Your firms are built on the Taylor model: even worse, so are your heads. With your bosses doing the thinking while the workers wield the screwdrivers, you're convinced deep down that this is the right way to run a business.
>
> 'For you, the essence of management is getting the ideas out of the heads of the bosses into the hands of labour. We are beyond the Taylor model. Business, we know, is now so complex and difficult, the survival of firms is hazardous in an environment that is increasingly unpredictable, competitive and fraught with danger, that their continued existence depends on the day-to-day mobilization of every ounce of intelligence.
>
> 'For us, the core of management is precisely this art of mobilizing and pulling together the intellectual resources of all employees in the service of the firm . . .'

Only by drawing on the combined brainpower of all its employees can a firm face up to the turbulence and constraints of today's environment.

His point was that when a Japanese organization of 100,000 employees was in competition with a Western one of the same size, the Japanese firm would be bound to win because it utilized the brainpower of all 100,000 people, whereas the Western company used only the brains of the 20,000 or so people called managers.

The message was clear – but it took several years and a great deal of painful learning before its implications dawned on Western companies. With typical gusto they seized on empowerment as the answer to all corporate woes. But what they didn't realize is that it is a lot easier said than done.

Making empowerment work

A large number of empowerment initiatives have not yielded the results expected. There are good reasons for this. For one thing, simply telling people they are empowered to make decisions does not mean they have the necessary support to do so.

Decisions require:

- resources (money, staff, etc.)
- authority
- information.

But there is another problem. In organizations where operational decisions have previously been made by middle managers and supervisors, it is unrealistic to expect them to give up that power overnight or for employees lower down to be ready to accept it.

In addition, before the empowerment bandwagon could build up a good head of steam it was overtaken by the downsizing bandwagon, which saw many companies stripping out layers of middle managers – the very people who were supposed to cascade decision-making under empowerment.

The result, in a lot of cases, was mixed messages, compounded by deep-rooted and often justified paranoia in the ranks of middle management. Not surprisingly, many empowerment initiatives were simply stopped in their tracks by middle managers who had no desire to give up their power at a time when they already felt threatened by redundancy.

In other cases, the wholesale removal of middle management meant that the handover of responsibilities was too abrupt, and the transfer of skills required to make empowerment successful simply didn't happen. In the most extreme cases, the effect was to hollow out the middle of the organization to create a decision-making vacuum at the heart of the organization, with no one prepared to pick up difficult issues.

Many companies failed to think it through. This was especially evident in terms of the failure to put the necessary supporting mechanisms in place or the will of senior management to drive the cultural change required to support the new 'can do' approach.

Few companies properly considered the implications for training, resourcing and rewarding their newly empowered workforces. Yet, giving people additional responsibilities suggests they should also enjoy:

- additional rewards
- additional training to cope with their new responsibilities
- a working environment or culture which is supportive of the change.

In most companies where empowerment has been introduced, one or more of these factors has been sadly lacking.

Dr Ian Cunningham, director of the Centre for the Study of Change notes:

'With the flattening of hierarchies, empowerment has become a fashionable term. In practice, it is often just a synonym for delegation. Instead of granting genuine power to their staff, managers remain as likely as ever to make the important decisions and only pass on relatively unimportant tasks to others.

'Delegation starts off as part of a manager's job which he or she then delegates. Empowerment, however, involves removing constraints which prevent someone doing their job as effectively as possible.'

EFFECTIVE EMPOWERMENT

In some areas, the empowerment movement has been effective. This is shown by the results of a recent survey (April 1997) carried out by the recruitment company Reed Employment.[2]

The survey sought to measure the discretionary authority of secretaries, or personal assistants as many are now known, over spending decisions. It found that nearly half of the secretaries surveyed in the UK had some degree of financial control; 44 per cent of secretaries in the survey could sign off money spent on a project on their own authority without asking for additional clearance from a manager.

Some 28 per cent could sign off up to £1,000 at their own discretion, 18 per cent either have higher limits or an unlimited amount which they could sign off on any one project without having to clear the decision with a manager. Moreover, 12 per cent of the total sample could sign off between £1,000 and £10,000 on one project, and some 2 per cent were able to sign off between £10,000 and £50,000.

Managers as facilitators

Those organizations which have made empowerment work have discovered that it requires a fundamental re-evaluation of the role of managers within the organization. In part, this is because their old decision-making powers are being dissipated to many more people, but also it is because the new culture to support empowerment requires a new way of managing people. That in turn requires a new set of management competencies and a new way of understanding what management is there for.

Belatedly in many cases, companies and commentators are now beginning to get to grips with what these changes really mean. So, for example, they are beginning to realize that the role of managers in future should be that of facilitator, coach and mentor – rather than decision-maker, boss, and policeman.

Learning organizations

Another fashionable idea among management commentators is that of the learning organization. The work of management academic Peter Senge has been influential in convincing companies that the ability to learn from the past is vital for success in the future. This means encouraging managers and other employees to experiment with new ideas and feed back the results to the organization.

But the point about culture is that whatever the official line, it is the underlying culture of the organization which sets the tone. Senior managers can talk about empowerment, employees taking the initiative and learning organizations until they are blue in the face, for all the good it will do if those behaviours are not supported by the culture.

In particular, managers are unlikely to voluntarily shoulder additional responsibilities if the message from the organization's culture is that the most likely outcome of putting their heads above the parapet is having them shot off.

One of the clearest indications of the decision-making culture of an organization is how tolerant it is of mistakes. To a large extent this will determine how willing managers are to take risks. It is also an important factor in whether the organization has the ability to learn.

Learning from mistakes

Soichiro Honda, the founder of Honda Motor Corporation, once said:

> *'Many people dream of success. To me success can only be achieved through repeated failure and introspection. In fact, success represents the 1 per cent of your work which results only from the 99 per cent that is called failure.'*[3]

Yet despite current thinking, which suggests that experimentation is vital for companies to remain vigorous, in many corporate cultures there is a very low tolerance for mistakes, and individuals' career prospects can be severely damaged if a creative decision goes wrong.

Blame cultures and gain cultures

Writing in *The Times*,[4] Susan MacDonald quotes behavioural psychologist Dr Peter Honey talking about the difference between blame cultures and gain cultures on the way that managers approach decisions.

> *'An intolerant attitude stifles creativity. If an employer harps on about the damage that has been done, the person responsible feels ashamed, embarrassed and angry, and concentrates not on doing*

better but on ways of covering up any future errors. This is a blame culture.

'*In a gain culture, the focus is on what went wrong and why, and the employer encourages the person responsible to discuss how changes can be made to limit the chances of the error occurring again.*'

Blame cultures are often those which perpetuate a 'hire and fire' style of management, whereas gain cultures in general are much more forgiving.

To test whether your organization has a blame or gain culture, answer the following question:

- are you encouraged to take risks or try new approaches when making decisions?

Then contrast your answer with the following question:

- how often do you tell your boss or subordinates when something you are handling at work has backfired – always, some of the time or only if you think they will find out before you can put it right or cover your tracks?

Your answers, especially if you have worked there for a while, are a good indication of the culture.

A few years ago, I came up with the diagrams shown in Figures 7.1 and 7.2.[5] When the flow chart in Figure 7.1 was first published, several people told me that they pinned it up on the noticeboard at work. Typical comments were: 'That's us, the sweep-it-under-the-carpet model of management is the one we follow here'. This suggests, to me at least, that flawed decision-making processes are embedded in many corporate cultures.

Managing mistakes

It is one of the absurdities of business life that the culture of most organizations encourages employees to hide their mistakes. As a result, the learning opportunities they provide are all too often missed so that the same, or similar errors are repeated over and over again by different individuals in the same company. Worse still, misjudgements and flawed decisions may be allowed to grow to gigantic proportions and to cause huge damage to the profitability and reputation of the business.

It might be supposed that the trend towards empowerment – whereby employees are given greater autonomy to manage their own work – and aspirations among some leading companies to become learning organi-

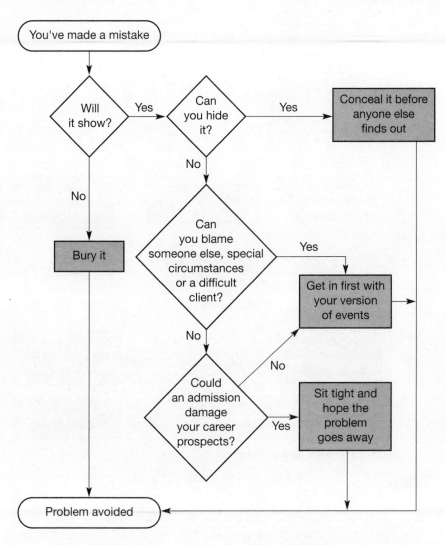

Figure 7.1 The sweep-it-under-the-carpet school of management

zations, and therefore better able to learn from their past experiences, would make it easier for managers to admit their mistakes. But the findings from a study carried out at Templeton College, at Oxford University, suggest that in most organizations this is not the case.

The study, by Keith Grint, a senior lecturer at Templeton, looked at the processes whereby organizations displace responsibility for decisions and managerial problems. His findings shed some light on the issue of mistake management and the way that bad decisions are often concealed.

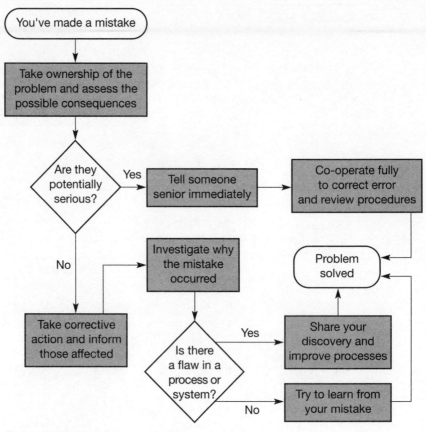

Figure 7.2 The learning organization

According to Grint:

> *'In most organizations there are no rewards for being a bearer of bad news. Managers who make it to the top of the organization are usually those who tell the managers above them what they want to hear. Even those organizations that have tried to introduce empowerment don't give managers and employees lower down sufficient rein to enable them to make mistakes and then to learn from them and make more mistakes. So mistakes, which should be a very powerful means of learning, are not.'*

Learning from failure

Errors, however, are not always the fault of the individual who makes them. In some instances they are caused by a flaw in the decision-making systems or processes by which the company operates. But unless they are acknowledged, nothing can be done to address the problem.

In his seminal book *The Fifth Discipline: The Art and Practice of the Learning Organization*, American management academic Peter Senge suggests that failure is an opportunity for learning.

Senge cites the example of Ed Land, founder and president of Polaroid, and inventor of instant photography who had a plaque on the wall of his office which read: 'A MISTAKE IS AN EVENT THE FULL BENEFIT OF WHICH HAS NOT YET BEEN TURNED TO YOUR ADVANTAGE'.[6]

Why then do we feel the need to hide our mistakes from others? Keith Grint says:

'British and American organizations in particular tend to combine the two elements of short-termism and a low trust culture. Typically, people in these sorts of organizations have less incentive to take responsibility for mistakes than those in higher trust cultures with longer time-scales such as Japanese and German companies.'

'Even where companies have tried to move away from bureaucracy by decentralizing authority and introducing empowerment, people remain risk-averse because they are sceptical. They know that if they raise their heads above by the parapet by admitting they've made a mistake they will have them shot off.'

Why mistakes are made

According to Dr Michael Pearn, a chartered occupational psychologist, most mistakes in decision-making are made because:

- a person does not agree with others about the goals to be achieved
- the information given out is confusing to those who have to act on it
- people are harassed through working under pressure.

One of the best ways for employees to learn from mistakes, he says, is to allow them to take responsibility for bad decisions, and map out their own solutions.

Groupthink

Groupthink is the name given to the way in which within a community of people ideas or a set of beliefs can take on a dynamic of their own and quickly turn into a type of dogma. The phenomenon is far from under-stood even by organizational behaviourists. What seems to happen is that once they achieve a certain critical mass, beliefs – whether validated or not – become 'accepted truths' within a culture which makes them difficult to challenge even when the conditions that gave rise to them alter.

Consequences of groupthink

The phenomenon of groupthink has been the cause of many a bad deci-sion. In some cases, it has led to mistakes of almost Biblical proportions. A famous example illustrates how difficult it is to halt a misguided pro-ject once it builds up a good head of steam.

The London Stock Exchange's belated decision to scrap the ill-fated computer project Taurus at a cost of £75 million was a classic case of a misconceived plan allowed to ricochet down the tracks simply because no-one involved was willing or able to admit the enormity of the mistake. As Widget Finn pointed out in *The Times*:

> *'Many informed people had reservations about Taurus, but they didn't want to be seen to question a project which seemed vital for London's financial status. A week after Taurus collapsed in 1993, no-one could think of a good reason why it had been installed in the first place.'*[7]

This problem is often compounded by a cultural intolerance for mistakes which is common to many organiz-ations. This reinforces one of the most damaging behaviours known to busi-ness: a preference for covering up problems. (See Chapter 9 for more on this.)

> **'The phenomenon of groupthink has been the cause of many a bad decision.'**

In general, groupthink poses a serious danger to effective decision-making. In particular, it can cause the following:

- inadequate exploration of the issues
- tendency to accept received wisdom of the group without challenging its validity
- over-reliance on biased supporting evidence (see information drift in Chapter 6)
- discussion constrained by group norms
- inability to think outside the box
- social pressure not to rock the boat

- failure to ask what could go wrong or to make contingency plans
- blindness to paradigm shifts
- the decision-making process is often little more than a case of 'going through the motions' to arrive at a predetermined outcome.

The value of a dissenting voice

One way to offset the impact of groupthink is to deliberately include a dissenting voice in the decision-making group. More enlightened leaders use this technique to encourage alternative options when faced with important decisions.

When he was CEO of Chrysler, for example, Lee Iacocca would often appoint a 'contrarian' at important meetings to make sure he had a dissenting voice present to put the other side of the argument. But other organizations are less receptive to criticism. Warren Bennis, the American management guru, says that seven out of ten executives in America's top companies do not speak up when they think the boss has got it wrong.

Managing groupthink

According to Helga Drummond: 'The challenge to management is to break the bonds of conformity without creating problems for deviants'.

Some useful tactics are:

- keep the group size manageable
- adopt a lively and unpredictable management style
- establish sub-groups
- assign individuals to specific tasks
- solicit members' private views
- include a dissenting voice or 'contrarian'.

Politics and personalities

One of the most significant influences on joint decisions is the status and personality of the managers involved. Research shows that in many organizations, deference to rank or status often prevents subordinates from speaking their minds.

As Helga Drummond observed in a recent interview in *The Times*, too, politics and personalities are the main barriers when a group of people fails to come to a decision.

> *'Individuals in the group have secret agendas, conflicting aims and varying responsibilities. Status makes the mixture even more complex. Senior people's opinion tends to carry more weight regardless of whether they are right or wrong, and their subordinates seek to please them by telling them what they want to hear. In any group the dominant personalities will also tend to influence the decision or get their own way regardless of the objective merits of the situation.'*

But adroit leadership, she says, can prevent the pushy members of a meeting from carrying the day, by bringing out the quieter or more junior members of the group and encouraging them to express their opinions.

New technology can also prevent those who talk the loudest and have the most stripes on their arms from dominating the decision-making process. One technique pioneered by Henley Management College, for example, uses IT to neutralize the impact of status among company managers participating in a decision so that everyone's opinion is give equal weight.

Each member of the group attending Henley's Decision Support Centre uses a computer terminal, and the session begins with an electronic brainstorming session during which everyone inputs their ideas anonymously. Members then comment on the results, vote on the outcome and after more discussion reach a consensus by voting.

2. NATIONAL CULTURES

Not so long ago commentators were predicting that the globalization of markets would create a breed of international managers. These giants of management, we were told, would bestride the business world, cutting through cultural diversity with a universal management tool-kit, which would allow them to make effective decisions regardless of the national culture. Companies have since found, however, that even their most tried and tested management formulae do not travel well.

The Japanese model of decision-making

It is often said that one of the important differences between Japanese and Western businesses is the way that decisions are made. Western companies – US and European companies in particular – typically make rapid decisions and view the decision as entirely separate from implementation.

Indeed, some Western managers pride themselves on the speed with which they make decisions compared to their Japanese counterparts. It wasn't until management writers such as Peter Drucker and others began pointing it out that Western business people began to realize there was something different about the way decisions were reached in the two cultures.[8] (Since then, many others have written about the differences between the Japanese and Western business cultures, but few have improved on Drucker's early observations.)

It wasn't simply that the Japanese were slow at making decisions – although it did sometimes seem that way to their impatient Western colleagues and business partners – it was something far more fundamental.

Put simply, in the West, the emphasis is on finding the right answer and moving on to implementation as speedily as possible. The Japanese, on the other hand, tend to place the emphasis on defining the right question. What they are especially good at is managing a process by which they reach a consensus on the need to make a decision about a particular issue. Once that consensus has been reached, it is possible to move quite quickly because there is broad agreement that a decision is needed.

In the West, we have cultural bias towards doing it the other way round. In other words, while we think we're faster at making decisions, what we are really doing is deciding on a solution – i.e., the right answer – and then trying to sell it to the organization. By the time the Japanese decide on the solution, the organization is already in agreement that a decision is needed. It's a classic case of 'less haste, more speed'.

Don't waste time on the wrong decisions

What it means in practice is that the Japanese don't waste as much time on 'the wrong decisions'. A famous quote from the American management writer Warren Bennis is relevant here. Bennis said that one of the most important differences between leaders and managers is that 'Managers do things right, but leaders do the right things.' Something similar can be said of ineffective and effective decision-makers – and organizations.

As Peter Drucker noted: 'Japanese managers may come up with the wrong answer to the problem, but they rarely come up with the right answer to the wrong problem. And that, as all decision-makers learn, is the most dangerous course, the irretrievably wrong decision.'

Drucker observed that the decision-making process in Japanese companies has a number of stages – each of which are crucial to the successful outcome of the decision. In the first place the focus is on what the decision is all about – i.e., what are the issues involved? At this stage, the aim is to bring out dissenting opinions and alternative ways of looking at the problem. The aim is to identify the 'alternatives' rather than find the 'right solution'.

This may seem a pedantic point, but it's not. Rather, it is to do with the frame of mind with which the two cultures approach a set of issues. This led Drucker to conclude that: 'Effective decisions do not grow out of consensus on the facts, but out of the clash of opinions and the understanding that flows from it. It is very difficult to reach agreement when two people are asking different questions.'

Ringi

The *ringi* process used by Japanese companies is vital to the way decisions are made. Proposals circulate within the organization and are initialled by agreeing participants. It is probably the best-known example of collectivist decision-making.

In Japanese companies, too, the decision-making process will also often suggest the level at which a decision should be made and may even identify the person or people who should make it. Most critical of all, the process eliminates the need to 'sell' the decision later. As such, it actually builds effective implementation into the decision-making process.

To illustrate the difference in the two approaches, Drucker offers the example of a US executive negotiating a licence agreement with a Japanese executive. The Westerner finds it difficult to understand why the Japanese keeps sending new groups of people who start what the Westerner thinks are negotiations as if they know nothing about what has been discussed before. One delegation is then succeeded six weeks later by another team from another part of the company who proceed as if they know nothing of what has gone before.

As Drucker explains, this is actually a sign that the Japanese take the matter seriously. They are trying to involve the people who will eventually have to put the agreement into practice. The aim is to obtain consensus that a licence is indeed needed. Only when all of these people have reached agreement on the need to make a decision will the decision be made to go ahead. It is only at this stage that the real negotiations start – and then the Japanese usually move with great speed. Says Drucker:

> 'When the Japanese reach the point we call a decision, they say they are in the "action stage". Now top management refers the decision to what the Japanese call the "appropriate people".'

▶

> By the time the 'decision' or action is finally agreed it will come as no surprise to the organization, and will meet little or no resistance. As a result, implementation is much faster. His observations of the way that Japanese companies operated compared to US companies also led Drucker to the conclusion that it was the difficulty of selling decisions to others in the organization that was the chief reason for their failure.

A new model

Fine then, you say, why don't Western companies just adopt the Japanese model? If only it were that simple, but of course things rarely are. The truth is that the Japanese decision-making process or model is specific to that culture. It relies on the cultural understandings and social systems which together make up the organization.

For one thing, most Western cultures are based on the principal of 'individualism' to a much greater extent than Eastern cultures. It would be untrue to say that the Japanese culture is based entirely on 'collectivism', especially today when Western influences are significant, yet that remains a very significant distinction between the two cultures.

Apart from that, there are also some problems with the Japanese model of decision-making. For one thing, as indicated earlier, it is an extremely effective way of reaching a consensus on big decisions, but it is slow and cumbersome for taking small or urgent decisions. (This, of course, can be seen as one of the great strengths of the Japanese model – that it encourages 'big decisions', which in turn encourage companies to take a long-term view.)

Why spend all that time deciding on a strategy that will last only a couple of years when by looking further ahead and being prepared to invest in the future you can set a strategy that will last a decade?

Or as Drucker puts it: 'Nothing causes so much trouble in an organization as a lot of small decisions.'

In general, the point is well made. But we all know that life isn't always that simple. For one thing, it is becoming increasingly difficult to predict what will happen in the next few months let alone the next ten years. In today's business world, threats and opportunities can come from the most unexpected directions – a fact that many companies have learned the hard way.

161

Living with cultural diversity

What the Japanese method of decision-making does teach us is that different national cultures have different ways of approaching decisions. This is something managers ignore at their peril.

Some of the most influential work in the area of cultural differences has been carried out by the Dutch management writer and consultant Fons Trompenaars.

According to Trompenaars, in every culture phenomena such as authority, bureaucracy, creativity, empowerment, verification and accountability are experienced in different ways. The fact that we use the same words often blinds us to the differences.

Trompenaars' research over more than 15 years – involving 15,000 employees in 50 countries – indicates the existence of four broad types of culture, giving rise to four styles of management: [9]

- the family
- the Eiffel Tower
- the guided missile
- the incubator.

Each has implications for decision-making.

The family model

This is typical of cultures as seemingly disparate as France, Italy, Japan and India. The result is a power-oriented corporate culture in which the leader is regarded as the caring head of the family who best knows what should be done and what is good for subordinates. Japanese companies recreate aspects of the traditional family. The idealized relationship is called *sempai-kokai*: that between an older and younger brother. The relationship to the company is long-term and devoted. The head of the family encourages discussion about issues and decisions, because that is the way he ensures agreement.

The Eiffel Tower model

Is typified by the approach of German companies where authority stems from the occupancy of a given role with prescribed decision-making powers and areas of accountability. Job specifications with clearly defined areas of responsibility form a superstructure within which the members of the organization operate. Each successive level in the hierarchy has a clear and demonstrable function of holding together the levels beneath it to maintain the management edifice. Subordinates obey not because of emotional ties reminiscent of a family, but because it is their role in the scheme of things to obey the person immediately above them.

The guided missile model

Is so-called because it is based on a view of the organization as a missile homing in on strategic objectives and targets. British companies as well as many American and Swedish companies are typical of this type of organization. The culture is oriented towards tasks and objectives, usually undertaken by teams or project groups. It differs from both the family and Eiffel Tower models because roles are not fixed. The overriding principle is to do whatever it takes to complete a task or reach a goal. This is reflected in the decision-making style which is often time- rather than issues-driven.

The incubator model

Finally, says Trompenaars, there is the incubator model. Typified by the new companies of California's Silicon Valley, such as the early days of Apple Computers. Distinctively Californian in their outlook, these organizations are structured around the fulfilment of the individual members' needs and aspirations. In this model, the management framework of the organization exists to free individuals from routine tasks so they can pursue creative activities. The only legitimate management function is to protect and enrich the efforts of individuals. These organizations are made up of knowledge workers who demand a high level of discretionary decision-making power.

Cultural interplay

It is where these four sets of cultural assumptions play against each other, says Trompenaars, that things can go wrong. Where problems occur it is often because the decision-making style or formula used does not take account of the different cultural values.

For example, he recounts the story of what happened at a management workshop.

'A Swedish manager complained about the difficulty of delegating authority to two engineers who worked for him – one French, the other Indian. In a discussion with other managers, the Swedish manager said he would like to solve the problem by making their objectives clearer at their yearly appraisals (his approach epitomized that of a manager from a guided missile culture); an American consultant present advised him instead to find ways to enrich their jobs (the incubator approach); while his German colleague argued that he should create clearer job descriptions and clarify their areas of responsibility (a classic Eiffel Tower approach). An Italian manager who was also present at the meeting, at first did not understand the problem and then suggested that the Swedish manager be moved to another post.

'None of the suggestions were without merit. But in the cultural context of the problem, the Italian manager probably had the best insight. The French and Indian engineers share with him the family-oriented cultural assumptions about their jobs. Put in this context, it is easy to see why they were unwilling to accept authority being delegated to them when the boss was around. Their cultural backgrounds dictate that it is only when the parent-figure is not there that the children will take charge.'

Culture clashes

Terry Brake, author of *The Global Leader* and president of the management and human resource consultancy TMA-USA, has also written extensively on the way cultural differences can affect decision-making.[10]

In an era of global business, he notes, contact among cultures is of more than anthropological interest. 'A clash of cultures affects the bottom line directly and can destroy a potentially rewarding joint venture or strategic alliance.'

The business press is full of stories in which highly successful companies have suddenly become grounded on the hidden sandbanks of international cultural differences. As Brake points out:

> *'On paper, Corning's joint venture with the Mexican glass manufacturer Vitro seemed made in heaven. Twenty-five months after it began, the marriage was over. Cultural clashes had eroded the potentially lucrative relationship.*

'What happened? American managers were continually frustrated by what they saw as the slowness of Mexican decision-making. Compared to the US, Mexico is a hierarchical culture and only top managers make important decisions. Loyalty to these managers is a very high priority in Mexico, and to try to work around them is definitely taboo. The less urgent Mexican approach to time made scheduling very difficult. The Mexicans thought the Americans wanted to move too fast, and vice versa. Communication was also problematic, and not simply because of language.

'American directness clashed with the indirectness of the Mexicans. The Americans often thought that the Mexican politeness was an attempt to hide problems and faults. Corning also thought Vitro's sales style was unaggressive. Over time, the differences were felt to be unbridgeable.

'Corning's experience is by no means unique. Disney's experience in France is another high-visibility example. EuroDisney was referred to in British and French newspapers as Corporate America's cultural Vietnam or Chernobyl.'

In another recent case, the sportswear manufacturer Nike withdrew a line of sports shoes. The original design included a motif which resembled the Arabic word for Allah, and was deemed disrespectful to people in the Arab world, especially as the shoes would inevitably become dirty. Clearly, the designers at Nike could have made an earlier decision to remove the offending emblem had they had a better understanding of that culture.

Procter & Gamble had a rocky start in Japan, too as Brake explains. Its decision to use an aggressive style of TV advertising (which knocked the competition) offended the Japanese taste for surface harmony, or *wa*, and damaged P&G's initial credibility.

Doug Reid, senior vice-president of human resources at Colgate-Palmolive, sees cultural sensitivity as perhaps *the* major issue to be addressed by global businesses.

'If you don't know how to manage relationships, you'll fail in most environments outside of the United States. The challenge is cultural sensitivity and understanding how things get done elsewhere. In some countries, government relationships are key. In others, sensitivity to the importance of the family is important. How you communicate – by constructive suggestions rather than direct orders – can make or break you. The business issues are very much the same around the world. When our people trip up overseas, it's over cultural sensitivity most of the time.'

165

Brake's culture prism

In his book *The Global Leader*, Brake offers a social and psychological prism to help understand other national cultures.

The culture prism offers a framework for understanding cultural differences. Each major group within the culture prism can be broken down into different pairs or triads of cultural preferences. The box gives a brief description of how one element – communication – can be viewed through the culture prism.

Communication: how individuals in the group express themselves

Implied: Meaning lies beneath the surface. Stresses empathy and shared understandings.

Stated: Meaning lies on the surface. Everything is expressed explicitly.

Circular: Maximum explanation of context.

Straight: Minimum explanation of context.

Ordered: Each situation has certain protocols that need to be followed: e.g., people do not speak out of turn.

Casual: Every situation is much like any other. Protocols get in the way of individual expression and honest communication.

The other elements break down in a similar way to communication. Taken together, the cultural prism can be used as a framework to help understand a particular culture and its possible interplay with another. So, if we take the Japanese and the Americans as an illustration, according to Brake:

> 'In Japan, communication tends to be implied rather than stated. "We stress shared understandings and empathy. We don't need to explain everything because we assume others will understand even before we finish speaking." This type of communication is common in cultures which stress the importance of group harmony and homogeneity over the individual. Indirect communication helps preserve surface harmony and avoid embarrassment.
>
> 'The Japanese also believe in circular communication (ringi). "When you ask us a question we will need to give you the com-

plete background to the problem so that you understand the context. Without the context, you will not be able to understand how we arrived at our conclusions. When we finish you will have a complete picture." (Such an approach is typical, too, of Latin American and Southern European countries.)'

Moreover, Brake notes that in Japan communication is very ordered. Each social situation has certain protocols that need to be followed; otherwise there will be confusion and misunderstanding. 'We feel comfortable when others conduct themselves in the manner appropriate to the situation.'

Americans, on the other hand, are more comfortable with stated communication. 'We do not assume you know what we want to say. We express everything.' Such a communication style is common in cultures that emphasize individuality over the group.

Americans also favour straight communication rather than providing all the context. 'When you ask us a question, we will point directly to an answer. We may lead you through a series of short, logical steps, but they will be concise. You don't need to understand all of the background to make sense of the conclusions. When we finish, you will have questions, and we will fill in the background as needed.' An American presentation or proposal, for instance, often starts with the bottom line and provides relatively little context.

> 'By using the culture prism as a starting point, managers can begin to assimilate an understanding of their own culture as well as others in which they make decisions.'

To Americans (and Australians, too) every situation is much like any other. Protocols get in the way of individual expression and real, honest communication. Americans try to side-step protocols whenever possible.

And so, as the culture prism demonstrates, communication between Japanese and American managers is fraught with dangers – something which is borne out by experience.

By using the culture prism as a starting point, managers can begin to assimilate an understanding of their own culture as well as others in which they make decisions. Useful as it is, however, as Brake himself observes:

'Ultimately it is only through reflection on our experiences and a deep respect – a sense of wonder, in fact – for other cultures that we can appreciate the miraculous diversity of the human race.'

References

1. Schein, E H, *Organizational Culture and Leadership*, Jossey-Bass, San Francisco, 1985.

2. Reed Employment survey, 1997.

3. Peters, T, *Thriving on Chaos*, Macmillan, London, 1987.

4. MacDonald, S, 'Blundering your way to the top', *The Times,* 20 March 1997.

5. Dearlove, D, 'Seeing the error of your ways', *The Times*, 19 August 1993.

6. Senge, P, *The Fifth Discipline: The art and practice of the learning organization*, Doubleday, New York, 1990.

7. Finn, W, 'Cutting out the indecision', *The Times*, 12 September 1996.

8. Drucker, Peter, *Management*, Penguin, 1979.

9. Trompenaars, Fons, *Riding the Waves of Culture*, Nicholas Brealey, 1993.

10. Brake, Terence, *The Global Leader*, Irwin, 1997.

Intuition and other 'soft skills'

'Once I have a feeling for the choices, I have no problem with the decisions.'
LOU GERSTNER, CEO of IBM

'Analysis is of less value when the focus shifts from machines to human systems and social terms because nothing is gained from dividing the whole into parts.'
CHARLES HAMPDEN-TURNER,
Judge School of Management, Cambridge University

Comments from top managers underline just how important intuition or instinct is in the boardroom. Take this comment from Sir David Simon, former chairman of BP: 'You don't have to discuss things. You can sense it. The tingle is as important as the intellect.'[1]

Or Disney chief Michael Eisner on his decision not to elevate Jeffrey Katzenberg to president, who said it was down to a 'lot of very logical reasons and also some intuitional reasons'.[2]

Virgin boss Richard Branson is another leader who seems willing to follow his instinct. Branson recalls his decision to go into the airline industry in 1984.

'It was a move which in pure economic terms everybody thought was mad, including my closest friends. But it was something which I felt we could bring something to that others were not bringing.'[3]

It should come as no surprise, however, that you won't find intuition on a business school syllabus. The reason for this is that intuition and other soft decision-making skills are difficult, some would say impossible, to teach. As a result, business schools tend to ignore the fact that these soft decision-making skills are a vital element of effective decision-making.

To be fair, some schools are now beginning to recognize other soft skills such as the ability to communicate with people as a key management compe-

'. . . intuition and other soft decision-making skills are difficult, some would say impossible, to teach.'

tence, but there is some way to go before intuition finds a place on the MBA curriculum. This is a pity, because without intuition, all that managers have to guide them is the cold, hard hand of logic, with its backward-looking analysis and limited horizons.

Even the most rational people cannot entirely ignore the powerful role of intuition in making decisions. Whether you attribute it to superstition, superior judgement, or the ability to read signs others have missed, the annals of business are full of stories about individuals and companies whose fortunes were founded on moments of pure and dazzling intuition.

In this chapter we look at the soft side of decision-making, including:

- intuition
- perception and judgement
- left and right brain decisions
- nurturing the inner sense
- tacit knowledge
- picking up signals others miss
- the heroic leadership myth
- counter-cyclical thinking
- decision-making personalities
- the Holy Trinity of decision-making – intuition, logic and experience
- hearts and minds.

INTUITION

To evaluate the role of intuition it is helpful to understand a bit more about how this mysterious human attribute works. The truth is that we don't really know, but we have some clues.

The psychologist Francis E Vaughan observed:

> 'At any given moment one is conscious of only a small section of what one knows. Intuition allows one to draw on that vast storehouse of unconscious knowledge that includes not only everything that one has experienced or learned either consciously or subliminally, but also the infinite reservoir of the collective or universal consciousness, in which individual separateness and ego boundaries are transcended.'[4]

When managers are asked what they think intuition is, they offer a wide variety of answers. Research carried out by Dr. Jagdish Parikh at IMD, the famous business school based in Lausanne in Switzerland, for example, involved asking 1,300 senior managers from nine different countries what they thought intuition was. Their answers can be grouped as shown in Table 8.1.[5]

Parikh's research also drew comparisons between countries (see Table 8.2). He found that Japanese managers said they used intuition most frequently in their work, a finding supported by other research into Japanese management.

Parikh gave American management the second highest rating for the use of intuition. The British came in third.

Table 8.1 Answers to the question: 'What is intuition?'

Description	%
Decision/perception without recourse to logical/rational methods	23.4
Inherent perception; inexplicable comprehension; a feeling that comes from within	17.1
Integration of previous experience; processing of accumulated information	16.8
Gut feeling	12.0
Decision/solution to problem, without complete data/facts	8.6
Sixth sense	7.4
Spontaneous perception/vision	7.3
Insight	6.7
Subconscious process	6.1
Instinct	5.7

Source: Jagdish Parikh, IMD

Table 8.2 Intuition rating by country

Country	%
Japan	45.8
USA	43.0
UK	41.5
Austria	37.1
Brazil	33.5
Netherlands	30.1
India	29.0
France	27.6
Sweden	18.8

Source: Jagdish Parikh, IMD

PERCEPTION AND JUDGEMENT

Scientists, too, have struggled to pinpoint exactly what intuition is. Most of the definitions they have come up with are flawed in one way or another. But one of the best efforts is that of the Swiss psychoanalyst Carl Jung, who said: 'Intuition is perception of the possibilities inherent in a situation.'[6]

Jung developed a model of two pairs of complementary mental functions:

1. **sensation and intuition, which he saw as functions of perception**
2. **and feeling and thinking, which he saw as functions of judgement.**

All four of these faculties are at work when we make decisions (see Figure 8.1).

Perception

Based on Jung's analysis, then, perception has two components – sensation and intuition, just as feeling and thinking are the two components of judgement.

Sensation is what we might recognize as information about our surroundings acquired through the five senses:

● sight ● sound ● smell ● touch ● and taste.

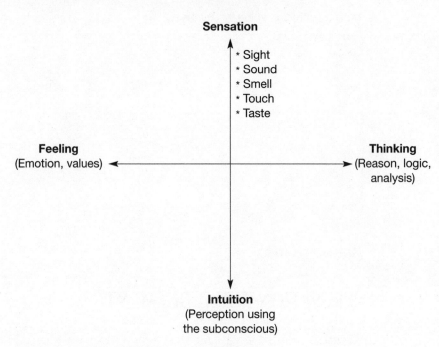

Figure 8.1 Jung's model of the mental functions

Intuition, on the other hand, is what we perceive using the unconscious. In other words, our senses tell us about the physical world as it really is; while intuition helps us understand realities that lie behind it. These include deeper relationships, patterns and potential.

No wonder, then, that intuition is so frequently cited as a key factor in breakthrough decisions. It may just be that intuition is the faculty that allows us to make the leap into the unknown; to make an association; or see a pattern where none has been seen before.

Judgement

We can take this a step further. According to Jung, thinking is rational judgement: giving meaning to what we perceive by using logic, analysis and argument.

Feeling, on the other hand, is a value judgement which we arrive at by using: emotion, morality, ethics or aesthetics to evaluate what is around us as pleasant or nasty, good or bad, beautiful or ugly.

Decisions, then, combine elements of both of these, as well as the two perception faculties.

Take Darwin, for example. A deeply religious man, his judgement alone would have prevented him from drawing the conclusions from his studies which resulted in the theory of evolution (indeed, his judgement led him to delay the publication of his findings for many years).

Yet Darwin somehow made the leap from his religious beliefs to the theory that changed the way human beings understand their place in Nature. In so doing, the voice in Darwin's head that would not be silenced was that of intuition. Against his better judgement, he perceived the pattern of evolution that manifested itself in the species he studied on the Galapagos Islands.

LEFT AND RIGHT BRAIN DECISIONS

The work of Roger Sperry in the 1960s and of others since has helped popularize the idea of 'right brain' and 'left brain' thinking. Most of what we understand about the differences between the two sides of the brain is greatly simplified, but it does provide a useful way to understand the operation of our different faculties.

Suffice it to say here that the right side of the brain is believed to be the centre for creative thoughts and emotions, while the left side is believed to be the logical problem-solving area of the brain. So left brain has come to be associated with: logic, language, reasoning, working with numbers, linearity, and analysis. While right brain is linked with: creating images, rhythm, spatial awareness, association of ideas, creativity, and lateral thinking.

One explanation for what is commonly called 'intuition' is that the creative right side of the brain starts working on a problem before the logical left side knows about it. (Dr Benjamin Libet, a psychologist at the University of San Francisco, has carried out experiments which indicate that the right side of the brain starts to seek information about four tenths of a second before we are aware of it.) This may explain why sometimes the right side of the brain comes up with a creative answer before the logical left brain even gets to work on it.

Interestingly, too, it has been shown that the right side of the brain gets drunk first. When the right brain is aroused in this way, it impedes the judgement of the left, causing slurred speech and impaired decision-making (something to take account of when deciding whether to drive home after a party).

The right brain also tends to shut down under stress in order to protect itself. Think of arriving at the scene of a road accident, for example – the imagination will be suppressed to allow the rational faculties to 'get on with what has to be done'.

As a lot of important decisions are made under stressful conditions, this is a point of some significance. It means that at the very time we need our right brain to come up with a creative solution, chances are that at that very time it is shutting up shop.

> 'One explanation for what is commonly called "intuition" is that the creative right side of the brain starts working on a problem before the logical left side knows about it.'

NURTURING THE INNER SENSE

In their excellent book on leadership, Randall P White, Philip Hodgson and Stuart Crainer write about the need for managers to develop and hone an 'inner sense'.[7] This inner sense, they say, takes in intuition, gut feeling, instinct and much more which managers fail to understand but utilize constantly in the course of their careers.

Despite this fact, they say, most executives are either unable or unwilling to acknowledge that their inner sense is what guides much of what they do, and the decisions they make.

'Most executives can't and won't talk about it. Shareholders and institutional investors are particularly unimpressed by intuitive decisions and judgements. As a result, annual reports and the like have become works of incredible fiction. If a chief executive hits on a brilliant idea while in the bath, it is not something he will proclaim at the AGM.

'The truth is that for all the flow charts, neat diagrams and carefully constructed hierarchies, no executive can escape or avoid inner sense. Indeed, with growing emphasis on the speed of decision-making, inner sense is likely to increase in importance.

'Management was once tangible (or so we were led to believe). And, when it wasn't, managers tried their damnedest to make it so. They produced reports, budgets, strategic plans, memos, directives, rules and minutes. It didn't work. There was – and is – something more. As we have seen, corporate life is more intangible than ever. The decisions are bigger, the information more complex and the time-scales shorter.'

They point to the rise of the knowledge worker as a sign that it is knowledge and not information that really counts in business today, yet much of what we think of as knowledge remains inextricably linked to hard facts. Mastering the inner sense, however, relies on being able to interpret 'tacit knowledge'.

They are not the only ones to claim that Western managers are more comfortable with facts than they are with feelings. In their book *The Knowledge-creating Company*, Ijkujiro Nonaka and Hirotaka Takeuchi, two Japanese academics, argue that Western companies remain caught up in 'explicit' knowledge while the Japanese thrive on 'tacit' knowledge.[8]

TACIT KNOWLEDGE

Tacit knowledge, say Nonaka and Takeuchi, is more elusive. It is based on gut feeling, idealism and skills. To fully utilize such knowledge, they advocate three elements.

- First, companies must ensure that employees share experiences. This revolves around shifting, flexible teams.

- Second, companies must use middle managers as a conduit of information between the factory floor and the boardroom, as this creates information flow.

- Third, they suggest that companies must structure themselves as 'hypertext' organizations. This unites the traditional hierarchy with freer creative teams which allows both to be based on a third common element – the tacit base of knowledge in the organization.

The tacit knowledge inventory

In their work on tacit knowledge, Richard Wagner and Robert Sternberg have developed what they describe as an inventory for managers.[9] They identify three types of tacit knowledge used by successful managers.

- *Tacit knowledge about managing oneself:* this refers to self-knowledge about what motivates you and the way you organize aspects of your management performance. An example of this is knowing the best way to overcome the problem of procrastination.

- *Tacit knowledge about managing others:* refers to knowledge about managing one's subordinates, peers and superiors. For example, knowing the best way to convince your boss that what you are proposing is a good idea.

- *Tacit knowledge about managing tasks:* refers to knowledge about how to do specific managerial tasks well. For example, knowing how to get your main point across when making a presentation.

PICKING UP SIGNALS OTHERS MISS

According to White, Hodgson and Crainer, one of the clearest uses of inner sense is picking up on suggestions, patterns and trends within the organization and in the marketplace.

> *'Executives make a great many decisions based on faint signals. Learning to adapt, to cope with the market and the environment is important – but that is learning about what is already there. The other kind of learning is an increased curiosity about what isn't yet there.'*

This, they say, involves 'seeking out faint signals.'

Sometimes, though, signals that seem faint to others, or perhaps just don't register, appear so loud to the intuitive decision-maker that to ignore them is impossible. With hindsight, the signals may seem obvious to all of us, but it is the antennae – or inner sense – of the decision-maker that makes them so.

Nurturing the inner sense is all about developing what White, Hodgson and Crainer call 'spectacular instincts'. Personally, I know of no better example of spectacular instincts than those shown by Tony Pidgley, managing director of the Berkeley Group in 1989 (see box).

CASE STUDY: THE BERKELEY GROUP

At the end of 1988, at the height of the property boom, Tony Pidgley, managing director of the house-building company the Berkeley Group made what has since been described as 'one of the finest commercial decisions ever made in this country'.

What Pidgely, a man who has built a company on quality of product and a remarkable instinct for the housing market, detected was the turning point in the boom to bust cycle. By reading what he calls 'the Indian signs'- faint signals to others but neon signs to Pidgley – he urged the company to 'go liquid' by converting all its land holdings and house stocks into cash as quickly as possible.

As he explained in a recent interview:

'We call it Indian science. Property is a feast or famine business. You buy at the bottom and sell at the top. If house prices are doubling, that's not normal business, that's hyperinflation. It's time to get out. It's good old-fashioned common sense, something we're good at. History shows us what happens if you don't make the right adjustments at the right time.

'In November 1988, we debated what to do. We have some assets put away in the cupboard for a rainy day, of course, all companies do. We felt that the market couldn't go on the way it was going. We felt we had to protect the assets of the business. On 1 February 1989 we announced it to the City and instructed the managing directors of all our businesses to go liquid.'

What is remarkable, too, is the speed and decisiveness with which the company acted. Normally the group allows a high degree of autonomy to its operating companies, allowing the managing directors to run their own show. But as Pidgley notes, what happened on 1 February 1989 was a special moment.

'That's probably the only time we've ever brought all the MDs together at one time. Normally we don't bring them together to

▶

▶

lecture them like some companies. We never summon them. All we do is set the margin for the group. But back in February 1989 we told them sell anything and everything. We knew that if we were wrong and had gone too early we might miss out on some profits, but if we went too late we could lose the business. We felt people were becoming too cavalier in the market.'

Pidgley was right. Because of his instincts the company weathered the recession much better than its rivals – many of which went bust or struggled to survive. As a result, City analysts now regard Berkeley as a bellwether for the property market.

Building intuition

White, Hodgson and Crainer offer the following advice for building intuition.

1. Find your own inner sense and listen to it. ('It is something that leaves you on a little razor edge all the time and makes you think that on the night it will be all right', says Dame Judi Dench, the actress.)

2. Acknowledge the existence and value of inner sense in others: can you learn anything from watching them in action? How they approach a problem or decision, for example.

3. Create an environment in which you can explore the first two issues.

And here is a checklist for gauging the strength of your own inner sense.

- *Are you on the lookout for the faintest of signals?*
- *Do you find it easy to make predictions for the future?*
- *Do you have a sixth sense about the correctness of a decision?*
- *Are you most at ease with familiar problems and decisions?*

An article in *The Economist*[10] on Bill Gates observed:

'His genius has never consisted in seeing further than anyone else, but in seeing the near future more clearly and understanding much better than his competitors how to exploit it. Time and time again, Microsoft has recognized the potential in someone else's idea and simply done it better.'

It helps, of course, if you have the sort of financial backing that Microsoft has to make things work, but it wasn't always so. Early on in its history, too, Bill Gates demonstrated his ability to read faint signals.

At that time, the giant mainframe computer companies IBM and Digital Equipment had all the facts at their fingertips. But it didn't help them spot the fact that the PC market was going to take off. Microsoft, though, picked up those faint signals. As Bill Gates told *Fortune* magazine[11] in 1995:

> 'I remember, from the very beginning, we wondered, "What would it mean for DEC once microcomputers were powerful and cheap enough? What would it mean for IBM?" To us it seemed they were screwed. We thought maybe they'd even be screwed tomorrow. We were saying "God how come these guys aren't stunned? How come they're not amazed and scared?" By the time we got to Albuquerque to start Microsoft in 1975, the notion was fairly clear to us that computers were going to be a big personal tool.'

THE HEROIC LEADERSHIP MYTH

Throughout the ages, leaders have exerted a fascination bordering on obsession. We have created a sort of mystique and myth around our most famous leaders with whom we regularly compare others.

Where once these heroic figures might have been drawn from the ranks of our military leaders, monarchs or politicians, however, recent years have seen us turn our eyes increasingly to the world of business. It is no coincidence, for example, that people such as Richard Branson, Sir John Harvey-Jones – and not forgetting Bill Gates himself – have become celebrities.

Part of that mystique and myth is the idea of the intuitive decision-maker who sees the issues more clearly than any of those around him or her and is able to dispense the wisdom of Solomon at the drop of a hat. (An idea reinforced by management writers who quote their wise words with reverence, as I did with Bill Gates just a moment ago). This has the rather unfortunate effect of convincing people that the ability to make effective decisions is something you are born with rather than a skill which can be improved through practise.

Managing the inner sense

Research carried out for the book *What Do High-performance Managers Really Do?*,[12] suggests that managers who use their inner sense effectively are likely to have a number of characteristics.

- They make decisions quickly and confidently. They are willing to back their judgement and don't spend large amounts of time weighing things up.
- They use data only when necessary.
- They recognize and use their inner sense as a skill, part of their management armoury.
- They accept and encourage ideas, whatever their source or apparent usefulness, at every stage.
- They act on intuitive judgements, rather than questioning them.
- They accept no rigid or wrong method of doing things. If something feels, looks or seems right, they will do it. (This is not to be confused with ethical judgements, discussed in the next chapter.)

COUNTER-CYCLICAL THINKING

One of the most valuable aspects of intuitive decision-making is that it allows us to see things others don't. The facts, such as they are, are likely to be available to the competition as well. But as the Microsoft example earlier indicates it is the application of intuition to those facts that makes the difference. It allows managers to act on their hunches.

It is clear that any decision that bucks conventional wisdom of the time – i.e., is counter-cyclical – stands to reap greater rewards if success-ful. (It may also have a greater chance of failure because it relies on predicting the turning point in a cycle or a moment of change.)

Buying shares when everyone else is selling them is a risky decision, unless you are sure the price is going to rise again in the near future. If you are sure that is the case, however, it is likely to be a highly profitable enterprise.

DECISION-MAKING PERSONALITIES

It is important to realize that people have different decision-making styles which favour certain faculties or thought processes. Scientists are still some way from a clear understanding of how thought processes work, but it is possible that in time they will be able to trace the route that ideas take as they move through the brain.

Until then, however, we will have to make do with generalizations.

Types of decision-maker

Using his observations and historical accounts, Harold Leavit invented a typology which divides decision-makers, leaders in particular, into three categories.[13]

- **Type 1:** Visionaries: bold, charismatic, original and often eccentric individuals. (They include Jesus Christ, Winston Churchill, and John F Kennedy.)

- **Type 2:** Logical thinkers/analysts: these are people who deal with numbers and facts rather than opinions – they can be characterized as rational, calculating and controlling. (They include Jimmy Carter and Harold Geneen.)

- **Type 3:** Doers: these people are concerned with fixing and implementing. (They include Lyndon Johnson, Eisenhower and Napoleon.)

Any one of these types can make an effective decision-maker under the right circumstances, but most people would agree that all three sets of characteristics have their limitations. Being versatile is often better.

If we take a soccer analogy, for example, a player with an amazing right foot can be lethal in certain positions, but a player who can use both feet and his head to equal effect is probably a more valuable asset.

Basing his theory on the work of Jung, Roger Dawson sees four different types of decision-making personalities – two which he sees as left-brained and two right-brained.[14] The other key factor in his model is whether the individual is assertive or not.

So, according to Dawson, the possible combinations give four types of decision-making personalities.

- **Pragmatic:** left-brained (unemotional) assertive. (No nonsense, just give me the facts.)

- **Analytical:** left-brained (unemotional) unassertive. (Information hungry, give me all the facts and nothing but the facts.)

- **Extrovert:** right-brained (emotional), assertive. (Don't bother me with the facts.)

- **Amiable:** right-brained (emotional), unassertive. (Give me the facts and I'll see how I feel about them.)

My own model is slightly different. It identifies five different types of decision-making styles.

- **Flamboyant decision-makers:** pride themselves on making bold decisions, often snap decisions.
- **Practical decision-makers:** pride themselves on making sensible, workable decisions.
- **Analytical decision-makers:** pride themselves on making logical decisions.
- **Defensive decision-makers:** prefer not to make decisions at all.
- **Creative decision-makers:** enjoy making decisions only if they can utilize new ideas and break new ground.

Whichever model you subscribe to, however, gaining an understanding of your preferred decision-making style and that of the people around you – whether colleagues, customers or competitors – can be extremely useful. For one thing it allows you to compensate for your own 'predetermined' style, enabling you to consult with people of other decision-making tendencies before reaching a conclusion.

It can also be invaluable when trying to influence the outcome of decisions made by others – whether making a presentation to the board, selling to clients, or looking for career advancement.

For example, if your boss is a flamboyant decision-maker (extrovert/ assertive) there is little point presenting him with a carefully researched and costed proposal as it won't get read. Much better to try to win him over with the boldness of the vision, all the better if it can be put to him that the idea was originally his.

The opposite is true of analytical decision-makers, while a defensive decision-maker is more likely to respond to your proposal if you spell out the threat if no action is taken. Creative decision-makers, on the other hand, are more likely to take an interest if you leave some holes in the proposal that they can fill; while practical decision-makers want reassurance that the plan has both feet firmly on the ground.

THE HOLY TRINITY OF DECISION-MAKING

Some managers rely almost entirely on gut feeling to make important decisions. Most, however, use a combination of head and heart to reach a judgement. Often, it is experience, the third side of the decision-making triangle (see Chapter 1), that bridges the gap and allows effective managers to reconcile the other two, intuition and logic. Experience pro-

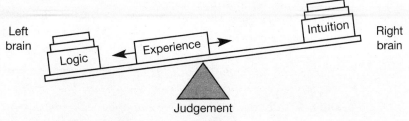

Left
brain

Right
brain

Figure 8.2 The see-saw of logic and intuition

vides the counterbalance that is essential to the most important faculty of all, the one which combines all three elements – judgement.

One way to think of this is as a see-saw where intuition and logic are at opposite ends and the weight of experience allows us to reach a point of balance – or judgement (see Figure 8.2).

The key to making effective decisions is striking the right balance between logic, intuition and experience. Managers, in particular, require all three elements if they are to handle the many different situations they face in their jobs. As Nobel Prize winner Herbert A Simon, professor of psychology at Carnegie Mellon University and a decision guru, observes.[15]

> *'Every manager needs to be able to analyze problems systematically. Every manager needs also to be able to respond to situations rapidly, a skill that requires cultivation of intuition and judgement over many years of experience and training.*
>
> *'The effective manager does not have the luxury of choosing between "analytic" and "intuitive" approaches to problems. Behaving like a manager means having command of the whole range of management skills and applying them as they become appropriate.'*

As Professor Simon suggests, the effective manager – or decision-maker – is not wedded to a particular approach, but is pragmatic. He or she recognizes the value of all three elements in the decision triangle and reaches a judgement about where the emphasis should be.

HEARTS AND MINDS

One other point about great leaders and decision-makers. The best decisions carry the hearts and minds of the people affected by them. Confucius refers to a Chinese guide to leadership:

'*Radical changes require adequate authority. A man must have an inner strength as well as influential position. What he does must correspond with a higher truth. If a*

> **'The best decisions carry the hearts and minds of the people affected by them.'**

revolution is not founded on such inner truth, the results are bad, and it has no success. For in the end, men will only support those undertakings which they feel to be instinctively just.'

No wonder, then, that so many 'downsizing' and other cynical management initiatives fail!

Great decision-makers

According to Roger Dawson, consultant and management writer, there are nine traits of great decision-makers.[16] These traits, he says, when combined with good decision-making habits produce effective decisions. The nine traits are:

- having a high tolerance for ambiguity
- having a well-ordered sense of priorities
- being a good listener
- always building consensus around a decision
- avoiding stereotypes
- always remaining resilient
- being comfortable with both soft and hard input
- being realistic about cost and difficulty
- avoiding decision minefields.

References

1. Hosking, P, 'The leader's leader', *Independent on Sunday*, 31 December 1995.

2. White, R P, Hodgson, P, and Crainer, S, *The Future of Leadership*, Pitman, 1996.

3. de Vries, M Kets, and Dick, R, *Branson's Virgin: The coming of age of a counter-cultural Enterprise*, INSEAD, Fontainebleau, 1995.

4. Vaughan, Francis E, quoted in *The Ultimate Book of Business Quotations*, Capstone, 1997.

5. Parikh, J, *Intuition: The new frontier of management*, Blackwell, Oxford, 1994.

6. Quoted in *How to be a Better Decision-maker*, Alan Barker, Kogan Page, 1996.

7. White, R P, Hodgson, P, and Crainer, S, *The Future of Leadership*, Pitman, 1996.

8. Nonaka, I, and Takeuchi, H, *The Knowledge-creating Company: How Japanese companies create the dynamics of innovation*, Oxford University Press, 1995.

9. Wagner, R, and Sternberg, R, 'Street Smarts', in *Measures of Leadership*, Clark, K, and Clark, M, (editors) Leadership Library of America, West Orange NJ, 1990.

10. *The Economist*, 25 November 1995.

11. Schlender, B, 'Bill Gates and Paul Allen talk', *Fortune*, 2 October 1995.

12. White, Randell P, *What Do High-performance Managers Really Do?*

13. Leavitt, Harold J, and Lipman Blumen, Jean, 'Hot Groups', *Harvard Business Review*, July 1995.

14. Dawson, Roger, *Make the Right Decision Every Time*, Nicholas Brealey, 1994.

15. Simon, Herbert A, *Making Management Decisions*, Academy of Management Executives, 1 February 1987.

16. Dawson, Roger, *Make the Right Decision Every Time*, Nicholas Brealey, 1994.

Tough decisions

'Decision of character will often give to an inferior mind command over a superior.'
UNKNOWN

'Business ethics are ordinary ethics applied to business. For a rule of thumb, anything you want to hide is probably not ethical.'
STANLEY KAIER, director of the Institute of Business Ethics

'If someone tells you he is going to make a "realistic decision", you immediately understand that he has resolved to do something bad.'
MARY MCCARTHY, American novelist

Some decisions are especially difficult – those involving redundancies, for example, or blowing the whistle on colleagues or employers. Often, however, these are the most important decisions a manager will face. This chapter looks at the moral and ethical dimension and offers a framework for making tough decisions, including:

- business ethics
- the range of ethical decisions
- grey areas
- creating an ethical framework for decisions
- ethical codes
- monitoring ethical performance
- ethical training
- knowing right from wrong
- corporate values
- stakeholders
- handling redundancies
- blowing the whistle (the toughest decision of all).

First, though, it is worth pausing to consider why ethical concerns are increasingly important to managers and organizations. For one thing, companies are under growing pressure from the media, government and public opinion to account for their actions and justify their decisions.

In America, for example, the *Federal Sentencing Guidelines* passed by Congress in 1991, state that companies without comprehensive ethics programmes in place are subject to fines up to 80 times the amount of the original penalty for violations of industry standards and regulations.

At the same time, many managers and employees are experiencing greater levels of responsibility and decision-making autonomy than ever before. Moreover, many of the checks and balances of the traditional management structure are being removed in favour of self-determination. The result is that the moral conduct of companies results more and more from the personal values and judgements of individual managers.

The negative side of this, is that many managers feel they are under increasing pressure to achieve their targets at any cost. Balancing the ethical and financial dimensions of key decisions is not always easy.

A recent survey of 4,000 US workers found that one third of employees felt pressured to engage in misconduct to achieve business objectives; the same number had observed misconduct at work during the year, but fewer than half had reported it to the company. As Michael Daigneault, whose Washington DC-based organization Ethics Resource Centre carried out the study, told *Fast Forward* magazine recently:[1]

> *'I think what affects many corporations today is a form of moral duality, where individuals will hang their ethics hat at the door and say, "Well, now I'm in a business setting, so I should act differently than I would with my seven-year-old". I think that for our culture that is ultimately a very dangerous practice.'*

The challenge for companies is to find ways to ensure that ethical behaviour is seen as a core value of the culture and is given priority in the decision-making process.

BUSINESS ETHICS

According to Jack Mahoney, Professor of Ethics at London Business School:

> *'The aim of business ethics is to integrate business and economic values into a wider view of the significance of and quality of human living at both individual and social levels.'*

A more practical interpretation from Stanley Kaier, director of the Institute of Business Ethics, is: 'Business ethics are ordinary ethics applied to business. For a rule of thumb, anything you want to hide is probably not ethical.'

As these definitions show, getting to grips with business ethics is actually more difficult than it at first appears. The whole area is problematic, not least because the goal-posts are continually moving. There was a time when companies might have considered that the law was the ultimate arbiter of ethical behaviour. However, it is generally accepted now that simply saying any action by a company that is not illegal is ethically acceptable will not wash.

> **'The challenge for companies is to find ways to ensure that ethical behaviour is seen as a core value of the culture and is given priority in the decision-making process.'**

Take the example of recruitment decisions. There is legislation in place to protect individuals from discrimination on the grounds of gender, race or because of disability, but most responsible employers would accept that ethical behaviour towards employees goes much further, and should encompass notions such as respect and dignity that cannot be legislated for.

In other areas, too, the legislative environment itself is increasingly onerous. Growing concern about environmental issues, for example, has led to a tightening of the legislative framework within which many companies have to operate. In some industries, the legal responsibilities in this area seem to increase year after year, requiring managers to stay on top of developments.

For these and other reasons – including growing media interest in issues such as executive salaries and performance bonuses – business ethics remains a nebulous area, and one which continues to evolve over time as our understanding of best practice and what is and is not acceptable behaviour on the part of companies shifts.

THE RANGE OF ETHICAL DECISIONS

Clearly, no responsible decision-maker should deliberately flout the law. Those who do deserve its full penalties. However, the number of decisions which, while legal, have a moral or ethical dimension is increasing. It is these 'grey areas' that we will focus on in this chapter.

Where unethical decisions are made it is typically because the grey areas have not been explored by managers. Often, this is because the culture does not encourage frank discussions of ethical issues. In many cases, too, it is the result of an internal culture that regards openness as potentially dangerous. This can also apply to illegal activities.

Some years ago now, a research project in the United States investigated what it called 'corporate deviance'. The research showed that senior managers who stray from the straight and narrow are frequently otherwise remarkably law-abiding citizens and often pillars of the local community. However, they have built up a wall between the morality that applies in their personal lives and that which applies in business.

What appears to happen is that the company becomes such a dominant part of the manager's life that his or her sense of moral values becomes distorted. If it is right for the company, it must be right for the community, becomes the logic underpinning decisions.

What the study also showed was that few of these managers act alone. They usually gather round them a coterie of equally committed people within the organization who reinforce each others' values. People who do not approve or might blow the whistle are excluded from the club – where the action is – making those within it even more close-knit. The club then develops a momentum of its own, becoming difficult or

193

impossible to stop. Recent years have seen a number of examples of this sort of behaviour among prominent British companies.

Scandals such as the Maxwell saga and the BCCI affair, however, have put business ethics firmly on the management agenda. The public outcry caused by these and other scandals has led to a much more serious attitude to ethical concerns. Indeed, business ethics are now a core part of many MBA programmes, and are the subject of a growing number of courses, conferences and seminars.

The range of issues that can give rise to ethical dilemmas is already extremely wide – and getting wider by the day. They range from outright illegal actions, such as fraud and embezzlement, to decisions that affect the environment, and other issues such as sexual harassment, questionable selling strategies, and conflicts of interest. Increasingly, too, issues that would once have been seen as outside the public domain, such as remuneration packages for top managers, require companies to exercise their moral judgement.

GREY AREAS

The current debate about the level of executive pay – the 'fat cats' row, to use the tabloid shorthand – is a prime example of the way that the ethical goal-posts move over time. As recently as a few years ago, the right of a company – even a publicly listed one – to determine the remuneration levels of its employees unchallenged was virtually unquestioned. Today, however, as a number of cases show, executive pay levels have become the focus of intense public and media scrutiny.

Recent events even suggest that this is an area where governments are prepared to get involved. The recent furore over the bonuses paid the directors of the National Lottery organizer Camelot, for example, saw Camelot's chairman receive a dressing-down from the national heritage secretary. Arguably, the National Lottery is a special case, but the public debate on top managers' pay is clearly moving against the unfettered right of companies to set pay levels.

Similarly, as Shell found to its cost with the Brent Spar platform, decisions about how to dispose of obsolete plant must now also take account not just of rational considerations about minimizing environmental damage, but also of emotive campaigns organized by environmental pressure groups. There can be little doubt either that in both Britain and America the ethical tide has now turned against the tobacco industry.

These are just some of the more high-profile examples of the way in which the ethical landscape facing companies changes over time.

Today, ethical considerations can result from any of the following (and a lot more besides):

- fraud (BCCI)
- environmental issues (Brent Spar)
- competition ('dirty tricks')
- pay ('fat cats')
- selling (mis-selling pensions)
- advertising (Benetton's controversial advertisements)
- health and safety
- redundancies
- corporate gifts and entertaining
- pricing (cartels)
- sponsorship (tobacco)
- suppliers (late payment of)
- exporting (to countries ruled by unacceptable regimes)
- importing (from countries using child labour)
- marketing promotions (Hoover's free flights promotion)
- R&D (genetics).

In fact, you'd be hard pushed to think of any business decision that could not have an ethical or moral dimension.

CREATING AN ETHICAL FRAMEWORK FOR DECISIONS

The examples mentioned above point up the need for companies to manage the internal ethical climate in which decisions are made. So what can organizations do to ensure that the decisions made by its people take account of ethical concerns?

> '. . . you'd be hard pushed to think of any business decision that could not have an ethical or moral dimension.'

There is no simple answer, nor is it likely that any company can totally eradicate the possibility of either wrongdoing – deliberate or by error – or getting itself in deep water with the media or public opinion. However, the senior management of any organization – and this applies just as much to public- and voluntary-sector organizations – has a duty to take what practical steps it can to promote and maintain an ethical decision-making framework.

The US educational organization, the Ethics Resource Centre, recommends the following 12 elements to develop a comprehensive ethics programme:[2]

1. vision statement
2. values statement
3. corporate code of ethics
4. ethics office/officer
5. ethics task force/committee
6. ethics communication strategy
7. ethics training
8. ethics helpline
9. measurements and rewards
10. system to monitor and track data
11. periodic evaluation
12. ethical leadership.

Many companies will feel this is taking things a bit far. But practical steps might include the following:

- setting a clear example
- publishing a code of ethics
- monitoring and discussing ethical performance
- appointing ethical champions
- creating effective channels for registering concerns
- supporting the ethical climate with training.

Top managers set the ethical agenda

It is well known that messages from on high are rarely taken seriously by those further down the organization unless senior managers 'walk the talk'. Yet, there is a common assumption by top management that merely talking about ethical behaviour is enough to get the message across. Far from it.

In many organizations there is a tendency to regard what is said publicly as little more than window-dressing for a hard-driving, 'take no prisoners' attitude in the boardroom. Where double standards are seen to apply to decisions made at the top, it is hardly surprising that they tend to run through the organization like the lettering in a stick of seaside rock.

▶

In reality, what many organizations do is produce fine words on ethical issues which are then put on a shelf somewhere, while the true culture drives managers to ever-greater efforts to generate the right numbers. Mission statements, for example, talk about providing an exciting but caring workplace; meanwhile the company works its managers half to death.

It is no wonder, then, that the message that comes down is 'get the numbers right any way you can, and if that involves bending the rules, that's OK as long as you don't get caught'.

However, 'do as I say, not as I do', is no longer a viable approach. As long ago as 1979, Richard Schubert, then vice-president of Bethlehem Steel, put the point well when he wrote:

> 'Management has to do more than establish a code of ethics. We have a primary responsibility to motivate and inspire employees to conduct themselves honestly and fairly. Starting at the top, we have to set the example for others to follow by acting in a morally proper way. We have to practise what we preach.'

ETHICAL CODES

Many organizations now have ethical codes and guidelines which provide a framework for difficult decisions. But ethical guidelines are not a new idea. As Lawrence B Chonko points out in his book *Ethical Decision-making in Marketing*, the following was written over 3,000 years ago:

> 'Do not have two differing weights in your bag – one heavy, one light. Do not have two differing measures in your house – one large, one small' (Deuteronomy 25: 13–14).[2]

In Confucianism, too, the concept of *Li* refers to the way things ought to be done. Confucius felt that people need models to guide their behaviour. *Li*, then, is a way of life provided by Confucius so that no-one would ever be in doubt about how to behave.

A formal code of ethics serves a number of purposes.

- It provides guidelines for managers and workers to follow when making decisions based on value judgements.
- It creates a formal obligation for everyone within the organization to take ethical issues into consideration in the course of their decisions. They know they have a formal duty to assess the consequences of

decisions and those of others against what is right in the eyes of the organization as laid down in the code of ethics.

- It provides a basis for on-going discussions about the nature of ethical behaviour. These sorts of discussion offer an excellent opportunity to explore grey areas.

Indeed, the very existence of an ethical code is a partial protection against unethical decisions in the sense that, like a written constitution, it gives people a higher authority to refer and defer to. Moreover, it legitimizes taking an issue outside of the immediate work team if the individual cannot resolve their doubts with their immediate boss. Decision-makers know, too, that they may be asked to demonstrate that their chosen course of action conforms with the principles set down in the code.

For example, Coca-Cola tells its employees in its ethical code of conduct:

'The guidelines contained in the code are of necessity broad principles. As a result, employees may from time to time need assistance in determining how the code applies to situations which confront them. Questions about the code's application to specific circumstances should be directed at an employee's supervisor or to the company's general counsel.'

In other words, if you can't resolve the problem satisfactorily with your immediate boss, there is another option and you have an obligation to pursue that alternative.

A code of ethics might usefully incorporate the following.

1. **An explanation of the need for guidelines and how to use them.**

2. **The role of individuals in maintaining the ethical climate and integrity of the organization in the following areas.**[3]

   - Behaviour towards people outside the organization:

     (a) clients and customers

     (b) suppliers

     (c) shareholders

     (d) the general public

     (e) the media.

   - Behaviour towards colleagues at work

   - Behaviour towards the organization and its:

     (a) property

     (b) time

(c) assets

(d) intellectual property and copyright.

- Policy on corporate hospitality and gifts
- Confidentiality
- Activities outside of work
- Conflicts of interest

3. What individuals should do if they are concerned about the behaviour of other people, company policy or decisions.

4. What the organization owes individuals in terms of its ethical behaviour towards them.

The code should be distributed to every employee. Regular discussion groups can also help clarify its meaning and explore issues and grey areas.

MONITORING ETHICAL PERFORMANCE

Often difficult in practice, monitoring helps to ensure that decisions take account of ethical dimensions. The American company Elmer Perkin, for example, requires all managers to sign a statement once a year confirming that they have not deviated from the ethical guidelines. The company conducts sample audits to check these statements are true. In doing so, it sends a clear message that it will uncover unethical behaviour and root it out.

ETHICAL TRAINING

A growing number of business schools now have business ethics on the curriculum. In North America at the last count there were over 500 business ethics courses taught on campuses, no fewer than 16 business ethics research centres and at least three journals dedicated to the subject. For all this activity, however, there is no concrete evidence that American managers are any clearer about their counterparts in other countries.

Writing in the *Harvard Business Review,* Andrew Stark, an assistant professor at Toronto University, suggests that, despite considerable interest in the subject, US managers remain largely bewildered by it.[4] It is not that managers dislike doing the right thing, he observes, simply that they lack practical advice on coping with the grey areas where competitive pressures can easily lead to unethical decisions.

The problem is that while most managers have a strong desire to behave ethically, they are given little preparation to help them deal with the sorts of ethical dilemmas they are likely to face when making decisions. Ethical training can help them in two critical areas.

1. **Enabling them to identify when an ethical dilemma is present. For example, they need to be able to:**

   - determine where and how conflicts of interest might arise
   - establish whether the dilemma is real or potential
   - understand and examine their attitudes and motivations
   - become sensitized to the nuances of ethical issues.

Role-playing exercises, where a number of hypothetical situations are analyzed and discussed by a group of managers or employees, for example, allow the ethical dimensions of a decision to be better understood. Such exercises can also provide a good vehicle to lead into real-life situations that people face in their jobs.

2. **Providing a decision-making framework for handling ethical concerns – something managers can refer to in order to help them think through what is ethically correct, or to put conflicts of interest between stakeholding groups into context.**

In an article in the Harvard Business Review in November/ December 1981, L Nash offers the following guidelines as a way to examine the ethics of business decisions.[5]

- Have you defined the problem correctly?
- How would you define the problem if you stood on the other side of the fence?
- How did this situation occur in the first place?
- To whom and to what do you give your loyalty as a person and as a member of the organization?
- What is your intention compared with the probable results?
- How does this intention compare with the probable results?
- Whom could your decision action injure?
- Can you discuss the problem with the affected parties before you make your decision?
- Are you confident that your decision will be as valid over a long period of time as it seems now?

- Could you disclose without qualm your decision or action to your boss, your president, the board of directors, your family, society as a whole?
- What is the symbolic potential of your action if understood? If misunderstood?
- Under what conditions would you allow exceptions to your stand?

These questions provide a useful tool for exploring the ethical dimensions of any decision. But managers also need an understanding of the ethical framework of the organization within which they are operating.

KNOWING RIGHT FROM WRONG

In the end, the strength of any ethical decision-making framework depends on managers knowing right from wrong. Most people have no problem when the issues are black and white, but the grey areas can cause problems. One solution is to encourage groups of managers and employees to discuss the ethical dimension of decisions.

CASE STUDY: LOCKHEED MARTIN

Some companies have found innovative ways of exploring ethical issues. For example, the aerospace company Lockheed Martin commissioned a board game based on the characters of Dilbert cartoonist Scott Adams. Called 'The Ethics Challenge', the game has been a big hit with employees ever since it was introduced in March 1997.

As Paul Haney, director of ethics and corporate compliance told *Fast Forward* magazine recently: 'It was a great alternative to an ethics training class, which can be a bit of a yawner'.

The point of the Challenge is for teams to pick the best decision for each of 50 business ethics-related case studies dealing with issues such as corporate theft, charging practices, and falsifying records.

CORPORATE VALUES

Some companies have institutionalized a set of values which provide a guiding star for managers making decisions. The British confectionery and beverages group Cadbury Schweppes, for example, has remained true to its guiding philosophy.

In 1976, its values were distilled into a document entitled *The character of the Company*, written by the then chairman Sir Adrian Cadbury. They involve a commitment to: competitive ability, quality, clear objectives, simplicity, openness and responsibility to employees, customers , suppliers and shareholders.

For its thousands of employees working in 190 countries around the world, those values provide a powerful cultural glue and a clear understanding of what the company stands for. So, for example, when Eastern and Central European markets opened up after the fall of the Berlin Wall, Cadbury managers knew – without reference to London – that unethical practices of any kind were not an option.

The company continues to see its reputation as a major source of competitive advantage.

STAKEHOLDERS

Other companies, too, encourage their managers to view issues in terms of how they affect not just profitability, but the different groups that have a stake in the company.

The notion of 'stakeholders' is one that has growing resonance for politicians. Tony Blair, in particular, has talked of creating a stakeholder society where all sections of the population are given a stake in the future. But the idea has been around for some time in the business world.

Many companies now explicitly recognize that their stakeholders extend far beyond just shareholders to include:

- employees
- customers
- suppliers
- the wider community in which they operate.

HANDLING REDUNDANCIES

Breaking the news to an employee that they no longer have a job – whether as a result of dismissal or redundancy – remains one of the last great management taboos. Perhaps that explains why so often it is handled badly.

In May 1996, 20,000 insurance workers were eating their breakfast when they heard on the radio that their companies were merging and 5,000 jobs were to go. In August of the same year, 7,000 other insurance employees heard – also over breakfast – that 1,700 jobs were to go.

Sadly, such occurrences are all too common. One trade union leader even coined the phrase, 'Rice Krispies redundancies', to describe the phenomenon. There is the infamous story, too, of the company announcing the names of employees who were losing their jobs over the company's tannoy system.

We have all heard – and in many cases witnessed – similar horror stories. Poorly managed terminations add to the distress – sometimes even trauma – experienced not just by the employee, but also by the manager whose unhappy task it is to break the bad news. Where they are mishandled, the sin of ineptitude is often mistaken for callousness on the part of managers and can seriously undermine the morale of remaining staff.

At a media company where cuts were deemed necessary, for example, one employee describes the reaction of the managers breaking the news:

> *'As soon as they've made someone redundant they always disappear for the rest of the day. They know that everyone will be talking about them and saying what bastards they are, so they keep out of the way for a while.'*

No-one yet has come up with an acceptable formula for deciding who should stay and who should go, when redundancies are necessary. The traditional 'last in, first out' approach is still used but does little to help the situation, other than provide a convenient excuse. Managers often have only a consultative role in the decision, which in the final analysis is made by the human resources department.

What does rest with the line managers, however, is the decision about how to handle breaking the bad news. This is no small decision. There is also a range of services available to help the organization manage the process and provide displaced workers with assistance in finding another job.

Outplacement

In recent years, a whole new industry has grown up to help support in-house HR professionals in their management of terminations. Outplacement – typically involving independent consultancies paid to provide counselling and advice to employees as part of their redundancy package – is now a respectable and, some would say, invaluable part of the process, and many employers rely on outplacement consultants to pick up the pieces.

As one outplacement counsellor explained recently:

> *'I might get a phone call on Friday to be available on Monday. The person affected will be asked to go to an off-site meeting first thing*

Monday morning and will probably spend the weekend going about their usual business with no idea of what awaits them. Come Monday, I'll be waiting outside a hotel in my car. Once they have been told, then they are mine. It's my job to help them deal with it.'

The onerous task of breaking the bad news, however, cannot be so easily outsourced, and those who have to do the dirty deed often find it deeply distressing. Indeed, even though they accept it goes with the job, many managers say it is **the** toughest situation they ever face in their professional lives. As one young manager put it: 'It's a dirty business, but someone's got to do it.'

Do it right

The decision to make someone redundant is often made by someone who doesn't even know the individual affected. But managers who implement these decisions have a duty to ensure termination interviews are handled both professionally and humanely. It is their decision about how to handle the situation that is often critical. In many ways, too, it is the decision that defines their professionalism and competence as a manger.

Do's and don'ts of 'release interviews'

Don't

- put it off until the last minute (if you're late it can greatly increase the distress for all concerned)
- try to busk it with no set plan
- assume they know what's coming
- beat around the bush
- crack jokes
- say you know how they feel (you don't)
- permit outside interruptions – from phone calls, etc.
- be surprised if they react emotionally (no reaction can also often indicate a state of shock)
- allow them to clutch at straws when you know full well the decision will not be reversed
- ignore their body language
- expect to be popular
- be surprised if you are upset by the experience.

▶
Do

- ask for/offer training in how to handle the interview
- prepare carefully
- think about the timing (some experts say that last thing Friday or first thing Monday are not good times as they can induce added stress)
- consider the best location for the interview (off-site, for example, or in the office?)
- have another manager present (especially important with dismissals)
- leave enough time and ensure there are no distractions
- have a programme and stick to it as far as possible
- get to the point quickly and make it clear
- give the reason – and ensure it is consistent with the message given to others
- move on to explain the package on offer and the next steps (possibly introducing an outplacement consultant)
- keep the discussion professional
- provide written materials to take away (they will not absorb a lot of what you tell them)
- be sensitive to 'special circumstances' – such as a recent bereavement or separation – which will require special treatment
- ensure they are protected from embarrassment or awkwardness with other employees
- take some professional pride in doing the job

BLOWING THE WHISTLE

Finally in this section, we look at what is probably the hardest decision of all. The decision to blow the whistle on colleagues you believe are acting unethically.

Most managers believe that they will never face such a decision. Let us hope they are right. But, as Michael's story indicates (see box), it is a dilemma that confronts a substantial minority of managers in Britain every year.

THE WHISTLEBLOWER'S STORY

This is a true story. Michael was a biochemist with a food whole-saler which supplied meat to a major supermarket. Shortly after joining the company, he became aware that rotten meat was being supplied to the supermarket in breach of health regulations and the supermarket's own quality standards. When he raised his concerns with managers he was told to mind his own business.[6]

Coming from an area of high unemployment and with a young family to support, he might have left it there, but Michael's con-science wouldn't allow that. Instead, he wrote anonymously to the supermarket. The supermarket investigated, found his concerns were well-founded and took action to prevent any further abuse.

Most people would agree that Michael did the right thing, but the story doesn't end there. It rarely does for whistleblowers. Con-fronted by his employer, Michael admitted that it was he who had provided the tip-off. He was immediately dismissed from his job. Like many others, he paid for his integrity with his job.

Michael's story was documented in the second annual report of Public Concern at Work, a British charity set up to advise whistle-blowers. It is typical of the sorts of moral dilemmas that face literally hundreds of employees in Britain every year. Some of those who blow the whistle such as civil servants Sarah Tisdall and Clive Ponting become household names, but the vast majority remain unsung heroes.

The fact is that time and time again these individuals perform a vital public service, often ruining their own careers as a result. Some-times, too, their actions cause embarrassment to politicians. One of the least well-known aspects of the 'arms to Iraq' affair, for example, is that a whistleblower from Matrix Churchill had warned the Government that the company was supplying weapons-making equipment to Saddam Hussein.

His letter, which Lord Justice Scott described as 'highly significant', was kept secret from ministers for over three years. But the letter played a crucial part in Michael Heseltine's initial refusal to sign a public interest immunity (PII) certificate. Warned by officials that once the trial began the whistleblower might well go to the press, Mr Heseltine's evidence to the Scott Inquiry made it clear that he was worried that if he signed the PII certificate he might be accused of par-ticipating in a cover up.

THE LYME BAY CANOE TRAGEDY

Joy Crawthorne, the instructor who blew the whistle on the Lyme Bay canoeing disaster, was one of several former whistleblowers who supported the Public Interest Disclosure Bill. Months before the tragedy in which four schoolchildren drowned, Ms Crawthorne resigned after her warnings that a disaster was waiting to happen were ignored. In 1994, her evidence led to the first ever conviction for corporate manslaughter in the UK.

Commenting on the bill (a private member's bill that ultimately failed to be passed by parliament), she said:

'If this law had been in force, those kids might now be alive. For my part, it would have given me the confidence to pursue my concerns with outside authorities who could have taken action to prevent the disaster.'

The price of principles

Many well-known whistleblowers have paid dearly for their disclosures. In 1984, for example, Sarah Tisdall, a junior clerk in the Civil Service, leaked details about the arrival of cruise missiles at Greenham Common to *The Guardian*. Although politically embarrassing to the government, the publication of the document was not a threat to national security. This, however, did not prevent Ms Tisdall from being convicted and imprisoned for six months under Section 2 of the Official Secrets Act.

In 1985, Clive Ponting, a senior civil servant in the Ministry of Defence, was also prosecuted under Section 2 for releasing papers dealing with the sinking of the Argentinian warship, the *General Belgrano* during the Falklands conflict. In Mr Ponting's case, however, the jury decided he had acted in the interests of the State and he was acquitted.

In America, Roger Boisjoly, who raised concerns about a potential icing problem with the Space Shuttle prior to its explosion, was demoted for his trouble; and Terry Smith whose book *Accounting for Growth* blew the whistle on creative accounting practices in the City, lost his job.[7]

Fortunately for Mr Smith, the resulting publicity helped the book become a bestseller and he has recently published a second book. Many others have found the experience leaves their career in tatters.

According to Marlene Winfield, a trustee of Public Concern at Work charity and author of a book on whistleblowing called *Minding Your*

Own Business, whistleblowers often act in the heat of the moment without thinking through the best way to resolve the problem or the long-term effects on their own careers.

> *'They have a tendency to plunge in head first without knowing the risks. As a neutral third party, what we do is listen and discuss all possible courses of action, the likely outcomes and the risks involved. But the final decision has to be the employee's. Our approach is two-pronged, as well as advising employees, we also provide advice to employers to help them improve their internal procedures so that people don't have to make these difficult decisions.'*

Funded by a grant from the Joseph Rowntree Charitable Trust and donations from employers, Public Concern at Work is a designated legal advice centre which means that people who contact it enjoy the same duty of confidentiality as they would with any other legal adviser. It also means that employees are not in breach of the terms of their employment contract.

According to Ms Winfield, however:

> *'In the vast majority of cases, nobody benefits from whistleblowing except perhaps a newspaper. The whistleblower often loses their job and the cover-up that follows public revelations usually prevents the organization putting its house in order quickly. The only satisfactory solution is to have internal channels which allow employees to raise concerns without fear of reprisals, and a receptive management culture which puts things right.'*

Checklist for whistleblowers

Those faced with the decision should think long and hard about the implications of going public. A checklist for the decision should include the following questions.

- Do you have hard evidence to support your claims?
- Are you focusing on the issues and not the personalities?
- Have you thought through the consequences for your career, and discussed them with your family?

And then the following actions.

1. If the issue involves a matter of public concern – illegal behaviour, risks to the safety of the public or other employees – call Public Concern at Work – the charity has a confidential helpline and will be able to advise you (telephone 0171-404 6609).

2. Use internal channels first. But protect yourself by:
   - using a senior manager or non-executive director as a sounding board – but make sure they are trustworthy
   - contacting an employment lawyer – you may be breaking the terms of your employment contract if you go public
   - gather evidence and keep records of telephone calls or meetings to substantiate your claims.

3. Take your concerns to an appropriate pressure group, your MP or if all else fails the media.

In the end, it is a manager's duty to do the right thing as a citizen. But don't expect any gratitude for it, because it is seldom forthcoming. It must be your decision.

References

1. 'Work Ethics', *Fast Forward*, the Tom Peters newsletter, June 1997.
2. Chonko, Lawrence B, *Ethical Decision-making in Marketing*, Sage, 1995.
3. Clutterbuck, David, and Dearlove, Des, 'The Charity as a Business', *Directory of Social Change*, 1996.
4. Stark, A, 'What's the matter with business ethics?', *Harvard Business Review*, May 1993.
5. Nash, L, 'Ethics Without the Sermon', *Harvard Business Review*, November/December 1981.
6. Dearlove, Des, 'For whom the whistle blows', *The Times*, 5 September 1996.
7. Smith, Terry, *Accounting for Growth*, Century Hutchinson, 1992.

Real decisions in practice

'The block of granite which was an obstacle in the pathway of the weak becomes a stepping stone in the pathway of the strong.'
THOMAS CARLYLE

'Success depends not only on what you do, brilliantly calculated though it may be, but on how others respond and act.'
STUART CRAINER

'We learn from experience but we never directly experience the consequences of many of our most important decisions.'
PETER SENGE

Today, managers face an ever-growing catalogue of decisions in their professional lives. A great many are specific to their company or industry, but others are common across sectors.

There is a growing awareness, too, that decisions that affect their own future can no longer be left to the organization they work for. Career and lifestyle decisions are now the responsibility of every one of us.

PUTTING IT ALL TOGETHER AND IMPLEMENTING IT

Making these decisions involves putting all the elements discussed in this book to work. More than that, it requires managers to accept and welcome the responsibility that comes with making decisions.

> 'Career decisions and lifestyle decisions are now the responsibility of every one of us.'

In this chapter we consider some of the more pressing decisions facing managers today. In particular:

- staffing decisions
- the issues involved in outsourcing
- outsourcing IT needs (with comments from real decision-makers)
- what the decision-makers said
- the decision-maker's route map
- career decisions
- lifestyle decisions
- 'downshifting'
- health decisions
- defending lifestyle decisions.

With all its dimensions, the decision to outsource IT needs, perhaps better than any other issue, highlights the inherent complexity involved with business decision-making in the 1990s. We also consider more personal concerns which can bring managers into conflict with the organizations they work for.

STAFFING DECISIONS

These days, decision-makers faced with staffing needs have a much wider range of options than ever before. In the past few years, a combination of a protracted recession and increasing global competition has led to a large number of costly redundancy exercises. As the economy picks up and companies find themselves facing skills shortages, one of the most important lessons must surely be the growing need for more flexible approaches to these decisions.

Yet the reaction of many companies seems to be simply to take on more full-time staff, thereby storing up more trouble for later. If there is one thing companies should have learned by now it is that the future is difficult to predict. As the demands of global competition intensify, the key to success is agility – the ability to react quickly to opportunities and threats. This requires companies with the ability to turn on a sixpence, acquire new competencies and shed unneeded capacity almost overnight, in order to optimize efficiency.

In future, recruitment decisions in particular require a wider view of the options. This is both to offer a more humane approach to the people who work for them and also to ensure that expenditure on severance packages is not allowed to undermine competitiveness. Today, there are many more options to consider. Among them, for example are:

> 'If there is one thing companies should have learned by now it is that the future is difficult to predict.'

- recruiting full-time staff (the traditional approach)
- outsourcing functions (everything from payroll administration to implementing entire IT strategies)
- temporary or freelance staff
- using consultants
- interim managers (experienced managers who work on short-term contracts).

Of these, the decision to outsource is especially relevant.

THE ISSUES INVOLVED IN OUTSOURCING

The idea behind outsourcing is as old as business itself. Basically, it is a response to the question 'Which areas of activity are central to our business, and which can be best be performed by external suppliers?' It arises from the recognition that no company can excel at everything. Areas involving competencies that are not central to what the business does are best left then to those who specialize in them.

What has changed in recent years, however, is the understanding of which functions can be sensibly removed from the core business and sourced from outside. In the past, for example, many administrative activities were seen as part and parcel of running the business. As a result, it simply didn't occur to companies to outsource areas such as payroll, delivery of finished goods, and secretarial services. That has now changed as it has become fashionable for companies to focus on their core activities – those which provide competitive advantage.

Outsourcing decisions – whether to, what to and who to – must be one of the most important facing any organization at present. Whether it is on a large or small scale, it is likely that every manager will face this decision at some point in his or her career.

One of the most complex outsourcing decisions involves the provision of the organization's IT needs. Because of the specialized and rapidly changing nature of technology, it is a decision which creates a great many headaches for those concerned.

There are several dimensions to the outsourcing decision. These include the following.

- **Striking the right balance between who gets the projected benefits:** in particular, how cost savings are divided between the company and the vendor requires careful consideration (all too often the bulk of the savings go in profits to the vendor or supplier of the outsourced services, as, for example, do the intellectual property rights from developing new technology).

- **Providing adequate protection if something goes wrong:** the risk of outsourcing is that the company is the one which suffers if employees from the supplier/vendor make a mistake. Adequate contractual protection is vital to protect the interests of the organization if, for example, the outsourced computer system fails. In some cases, inadequate safeguards can even put lives at risk, as the example of the London Ambulance Service illustrates.

215

- **Managing redundancies:** what happens to employees whose jobs are replaced by the outsourcing arrangement? Typically, part of the cost savings from outsourcing result from reduced headcount. This introduces an emotional dimension to the decision. The cost of redundancies should be carefully factored into the calculations to allow for a humane solution. Failure to do so can also result in additional costs – including legal fees.

- **Loss of capacity:** the inevitable result of outsourcing is a reduction in the in-house capability of the host organization to carry out the outsourced activity. This can have important implications for the future if the decision is reversed or if the outsourced activity becomes core to the business further down the road. It can also result in the company missing out on important developments or strategic options later.

- **Agreeing service levels that meet the organization's immediate and projected needs:** whatever performance measures are used, service levels need to take account of likely improvements required to remain competitive. Customers' expectations are continually rising. With insufficient flexibility built into contracts, re-negotiating service levels to keep pace with market demands can be extremely expensive. For example, 48-hour delivery may be acceptable to customers now, but if a competitor offers same day delivery, the company will have to upgrade its own service offering.

- **Agreeing the implications of moving to new technology if required** (it will be at some point, after all). Failure to reach agreement on this can be very expensive.

Location of decision

In a recent Institute of Employment Studies report on outsourcing, Peter Reilly and Penny Tamkin suggest that the location of outsourcing decisions should be based on the locus of decision-making.

> 'Where there is a strategic approach to outsourcing, senior corporate management is likely to be involved; whereas where judgements are more pragmatic decisions may be taken at the operational level.'[1]

They offer the diagram shown in Figure 10.1 as an outsourcing decision tree.

Even those companies which have made a decision to contract out their IT systems will need to periodically review that decision, and possibly change suppliers, or even take control back in-house.

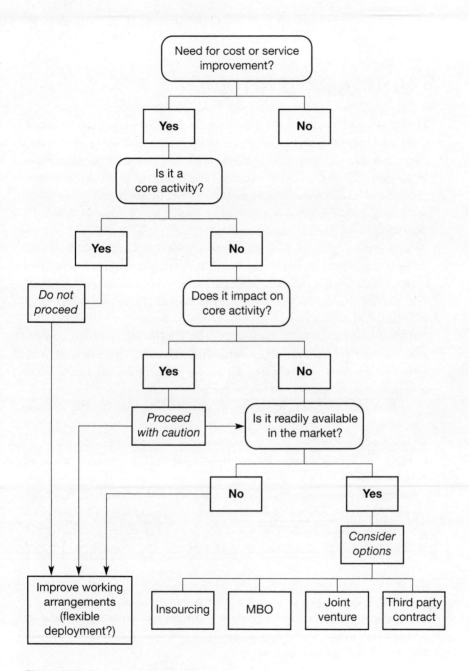

Figure 10.1 An outsourcing decision tree

Source: Institute of Employment Studies

217

With very large sums of money involved and often the entire IT infrastructure of the organization at stake, outsourcing IT in particular can be a nightmare for decision-makers.

OUTSOURCING IT NEEDS

In recent years, many companies have made the decision to outsource their information technology needs. Mary Lacity and Leslie Willcocks, two academics at Oxford University, link the move to a decision made by Eastman Kodak in 1989.[2] At that time, Eastman Kodak turned over the bulk of its IT operations to three outsourcing partners. In so doing, say Lacity and Willcocks, it triggered an important change in the way IT operations were carried out.

Senior management in other *Fortune 500* companies followed suit and signed long-term contracts worth hundreds of millions of dollars with IT outsourcing partners. Among them were: Continental Airlines, Continental Bank, Enron, First City, General Dynamics, McDonnel Douglas, and Xerox.

In the UK, too, similar outsourcing deals followed involving companies such as British Petroleum, British Aerospace, and British Home Stores, and central government departments including the Inland Revenue and the Department of Social Security.

In fact, so rapid was the move to outsourcing that by 1994, some 51 per cent of UK organizations were outsourcing some part of their IT needs. In the public sector, this trend was encouraged by the government's compulsory competitive tendering initiatives and privatization policies.

In the intervening period, say Lacity and Willcocks, there has been ample time to assess whether the decisions to outsource IT have been justified by the results. Over a three-year period, they carried out extensive research of a number of IT sourcing decisions in 40 US and UK companies.

Of 61 IT outsourcing decisions, they suggest, 34 (56 per cent) were successful, 14 (23 per cent) were unsuccessful, and in 13 cases (21 per cent) it was too early to tell. (For the purposes of evaluating the impact of these decisions, the key success indicator was defined in terms of 'achieving anticipated cost savings').

Why outsource IT?

There are several reasons IT in particular lends itself to external sourcing. Among them:

- IT is a specialized area that requires high levels of competence and constant training to stay abreast of developments
- IT requires very high levels of investment in equipment and software which quickly becomes obsolete
- for most companies, IT has an 'enabling' role rather than a primary impact on the business
- IT requires periodic injections of highly specialized skills which are in short supply and which are expensive to keep on the payroll
- specialists themselves may only be required for short periods of time and represent a drain on resources when they are not fully employed
- companies which specialize in IT enjoy substantial economies of scale which are not available to non-IT companies.

Outsourcing decisions

In total Lacity and Willcocks identified 16 sourcing intentions – covering financial, business, technical and political aspects. These were to:

- reduce costs
- improve cost control, including the introduction of better chargeback systems to reduce overdemand
- reallocate IT spending from capital to operating budgets
- allow staff to focus on core competencies
- comply with government-enforced market testing
- cope with IT burden caused by multiple mergers and acquisitions
- improve technical service levels
- draw on new technologies
- redeploy internal IT staff in other activities
- downsize
- demonstrate efficiency (get free benchmarking)
- play 'good corporate citizen'
- eliminate an IT development perceived as problematic

▶

- expose exaggerated claims by in-house IT departments
- jump on the bandwagon ('everyone is doing it')
- justify new IT resources.

From over 1,200 pages of interview transcripts, they identified seven important variables which affect the outcome of the outsourcing decision. These are:

- scope
- decision-makers (senior managers/IT managers)
- evaluation process
- scale of operations
- contract length
- contract type
- contract date.

Their research suggests key lessons for managing the outsourcing decision. These can be summarized as follows.

- **Right sourcing is selective sourcing:** given the diversity of IT operations in most organizations, no one supplier is likely to offer all the answers. Success therefore depends on a great deal of management attention, adequate protection, and a willingness to work towards mutual benefits.

- **Tailored contracts are better than 'strategic' partnerships:** too often the rhetoric of strategic partnership fails to translate into contractual terms, which should reflect shared risk and rewards. As a result, many such agreements favour the vendor. Tailored contracts – which explicitly recognize shared goals – are more likely to result in benefits on both sides.

- **Short-term contracts are better than long-term contracts:** short-term contracts have three important advantages for the purchaser: first, the pace of change in both technology and business conditions is difficult to predict more than three years in advance; second, they keep vendors on their toes because they know that failure to perform could result in losing the contract; third, short-term contracts allow companies to recover and learn more quickly from mistakes.

- **Outsourcing often involves substantial hidden costs:** unanticipated costs were a recurring feature of many of the deals studied. These often result from weaknesses in evaluation prior to signing contracts. In many cases, the company finds itself paying for the learning curve of the vendor, locked into old technologies with high switching costs, or incurring large discretionary spending outside the contract which is necessary to maintain service levels.

- **Internal IT departments should be encouraged to bid against external suppliers:** senior managers often exclude internal IT departments from the bidding process. Many believe that: 'If my IT managers could do it, they would have done it already'. Yet many IT managers are held back from introducing the changes needed to improve efficiency such as consolidating data centres, standardizing software, or implementing cost chargeback systems. Issues which are then waived when external vendors appear on the scene.

- **Sourcing should be decided jointly by senior management and IT managers:** success depends on working with those within the company. Senior managers can provide the larger business perspective and the muscle to enforce changes. But IT managers have a vital role in areas such as setting service standards, performance measures, and rates of technical obsolescence, as well as the general workability of the contract.

A number of comments from the report are also highly instructive. In particular, Lacity and Willcocks observe:

- *'All sourcing decisions should begin with the perception of IT as a business enabler . . . the power of information technology lies fundamentally in its integration with business operations.*

- *'No one vendor or internal IT department possesses the expertise and economies of scale to perform all IT activities most efficiently.*

- *'How do you assess intangibles like advice, courteous service, and environmental scanning?*

- *'It is important to ensure that the vendor gains a reasonable profit. Not doing so may trigger vendor opportunism.*

- *'Some companies have paid out huge sums to extricate themselves from contracts and re-build their in-house capability.*

- *'Internal politics often prevent IT managers from replicating practices used by vendors.'*

What the decision-makers said

Perhaps most illuminating of all, however, are comments from those involved in the decision-making process.

'A user will sign one or two of these contracts during his/her career: vendors sign one or two a week.' IT director.

221

'Once you sign with a vendor, you have no options other than con-tract terms ... if these are onerous when you get into that situation it's a lose–lose for both parties. What are you going to do? Sue them? Fire them? Stop buying services?' Chief financial officer of a major airline after signing a ten-year deal.

THE DECISION-MAKER'S ROUTE MAP

From the above, it should be clear just how difficult outsourcing deci-sions can be. However, we can also see how the areas covered in earlier chapters come together to provide a useful framework which forms the starting point for even this complex issue. So, a checklist looks like this.

- **What sort of decision are we talking about?**
  - **Is it strategic, operational or does it combine elements of both?**
  - **Is it a big or small decision?**
  - **Is it a money decision or a people decision?**

- **At what point does the decision reach the point of no return?**
  - **Senior management sign-off?**
  - **Signing the contract?**

- **Which model of decision-making applies? Garbage can? Game theory?**

- **Are there tools which can help us understand the implications of this decision?**
  - **Scenario planning, for example?**

- **What are the important time-scales?**
  - **When do we need to make a decision by?**
  - **How long should we be bound by that decision (length of contract)?**

- **Who should be involved in the decision-making process?**
  - **Senior mangers only?**
  - **Senior managers plus IT managers?**
  - **Others such as front-line staff who will use the system?**

- **Given the decision-making structure and culture of this organization, what is the best way to ensure the right people are involved?**
  - **Committee**
  - **Task force**
  - **Project team?**

- Do we have the right information to make this decision?

  - Does it exist?
  - Have we defined what we are trying to achieve clearly?
  - Do others involved in the process agree with this definition?
  - Do we understand what is being offered? Do we need to consult our own IT people more closely?
  - Do we need more information about the vendor?
  - Should we talk to other companies that have signed contracts with them?

- Are we suffering from information drift?

  - How can we compensate for that?
  - How can we test the information we have for bias?

- Do the numbers add up?

  - Have we taken account of hidden costs?
  - Is there enough flexibility built into service levels?
  - How much will it cost us to upgrade the technology later?
  - What percentage of the cost will be borne by us?

- What does our intuition tell us about:

  - the logic of outsourcing?
  - the vendor?
  - does it feel right?

- Are there any ethical dimensions to this decision?

  - Have we made adequate allowance for redundancies?
  - Are we sure there is no conflict of interest with the vendor? Does the vendor supply/plan to supply competitors?
  - If the outsourced system fails will it put lives at risk? Will it jeopardize our relationship with customers?

- What can go wrong?

  - Have we allowed for teething problems?
  - How easily can we get out of this if it's a disaster?
  - Are we missing something really important?
  - What is the worst thing that can happen?

- Do we understand the special characteristics of the outsourcing decision?

CASE STUDY A

Under competitive pressure, senior management at a glass and plastics company devolved head office work to business units. In the IT section the ageing mainframe and client-server development, together with most of the 45 staff, were outsourced to the same vendor on an initial two-year contract. The risks were recognized and explicitly managed. Business knowledge, IT strategy and contract management capability were kept in-house.

A short contract with the probability of further work, if successful, provided leverage for the client. The ex-IT manager became the vendor's account manager, thus securing the relationship.

The vendor was responsible for developing local area networks, but the client owned the assets produced. Former staff of the client were employed on the contract, but with their contribution enhanced by technical expertise from the vendor. The contract was delivered successfully with savings of £1.25 million and was subsequently re-negotiated for a further three years.

The CIO commented: 'Some of our other operations have gone into longer-term contracts and we have reservations about them. You are seeing terrific changes in information technology and information systems. In any case, we wanted to retain a certain amount of negotiating independence on the back of that change.'

'To support this, a very important aspect of what we were doing was certainly not to outsource control, direction and strategy. Those, we feel very strongly, have to remain in-house.'

Source: Lacity, M, and Willcocks, L, (1996), *Best Practices in I.T. Sourcing*, Oxford Research Briefings, Templeton College, Oxford.

CASE STUDY B

Senior executives at a chemical company signed a seven-year, comprehensive outsourcing deal, which treated the entire IT function as a commodity. They chose a particular vendor partly because its representatives promised access to specialized systems used by other chemical company customers.

Because these representatives presented themselves as 'partners', senior executives from the chemical company omitted contract negotiations and hastily signed an incomplete contract.

One month into the contract, the vendor's excess charges for items not covered in the contract were exceeding the fixed monthly

▶ price. As time went on, promises of access to additional software failed to materialize, and instead the chemical company had to pay the vendor to build new systems.

When these systems were late and over-priced, the company opted for cheaper PC-based solutions, funded through discretionary funds. Finally, rather than continue the partnership with the out-sourcing vendor, senior executives paid a stiff penalty fee to terminate the contract, purchased hardware and software, and hired a new IT staff of 40 people.

Despite the undisclosed additional costs – which the IT director characterized as 'embarrassing' – senior management believes the comparative IT costs will be lower in the long run.

Source: Lacity, M, and Willcocks, L, (1996), *Best Practices in I.T. Sourcing*, Oxford Research Briefings, Templeton College, Oxford.

CAREER DECISIONS

The other side of the staffing – and outsourcing – coin for many managers is the diminishing number of jobs for life. One manager joined a blue-chip company straight from university and worked there for 20 years. In 1996, aged 46, he found himself leaving the company, unsure what he would do next. Like many others, he had followed the classic career advice of the time only to find that his decision to stay with one company made him less attractive to employers than someone who has moved around. He observed:

> *'In retrospect, it would probably have been better for me to have moved at an earlier stage in my career. When you are at a company for a long time – even a very good company – your skills tend to be taken for granted. As a result, your value is undermined. A background at a single company is less marketable.'*

In the turbulent job market of the 1990s, a growing number of managers are finding that a career with a single company can actually be dangerous. Today, single-company careers are more likely to be viewed as limited and limiting. When the time comes to move, the initial shock of displacement is often followed by the discovery that potential employers view them as a poor prospect, with a question mark over their breadth of experience and adaptability.

It is an issue that is becoming increasingly common, according to out-placement specialists Sanders & Sidney. Says Ralph Carver, a senior consultant at the company:

'Join a blue chip company and sit there: that was the classic career advice. Now that's been turned on its head. The advice today is to take control and make your own career decisions – don't leave it to some benevolent HR department.'

Deciding when to move

According to Professor Shaun Tyson from Cranfield School of Management, managers must increasingly build careers between organizations, where experience is gained to be displayed like campaign medals on the CV.

'One thing that has changed completely is the notion of total commitment to the company because that cannot be reciprocated. It would be very foolish to put all your eggs in one basket.

'The question is what are companies looking for now? Many are no longer looking for life-time service. The company man ethos is disappearing. The sad thing is that people who bought into the message on loyalty and stayed now find themselves out of a job.

'The advice now is keep a weather eye open all the time. Companies are opportunists, you have to be the same. Think of yourself as a business – develop your own personal assets – skills and experiences with which you build your CV. You have to build and manage contacts both inside and outside the organization. It's very important, too, to have a good 'career story': one that is convincing.'

Adds another manager ruefully:

'I would still say that if you have the chance to join a blue chip company, then do so. But when your career progression starts faltering, think very hard about how long you should persevere. The lesson for me is that I was too patient. After some early career successes, I waited too long for things to improve. I regret that I didn't make the decision to leave earlier.'

Knowing your worth

These days, there is much talk in business about leverage of one kind or another. For the ambitious manager, there is no more important lever than knowing their perceived value to the organization. It is not simply a matter of applying pressure for promotion or a pay increase, however, it is about knowing which cards you hold and when to play them.

When it comes to negotiating a salary increase or a new career opportunity, timing is all-important, says Helen Murlis, senior director at Hay Management Consultants and an expert on remuneration.

'It's very important to keep your ear to the ground to know what your competencies are and the jobs you can do. But it's actually quite a difficult thing for individuals to do.

'People don't work for money alone – but it helps, especially if you feel undervalued or exploited. But bringing the subject up at the wrong time could be seen as ill judged; managers are paid to use good judgement, so this could cast a shadow.

'You're strongest when you've just been approached by a head-hunter or are receiving regular calls from headhunters. That's a good indicator of your market worth. The best time to do a tough negotiation, though. is probably when you've delivered a result that's extraordinary.'

Remember, too, that the days when simply keeping your head down was a sensible career strategy are long gone. From a promotion perspective – or a survival one for that matter – it is imperative today to be seen to be adding value to the organization, rather than simply keeping the wheels turning.

In an article entitled 'A manifesto for middle managers', management guru Tom Peters advises middle managers: 'If you can't put it on your CV, you shouldn't be doing it.'

> **'. . . it is imperative today to be seen to be adding value to the organization, rather than simply keeping the wheels turning.'**

What you can do to communicate your real value to the organization

The experts recommend the following tips.

- Keep a record of any business you have won, either directly or indirectly (keep track of leads passed to others), together with positive comments made by customers, suppliers and intermediaries.

- Make sure you receive regular appraisals to give you feedback on your performance and to set key objectives for the future. You may be working to high standards but focusing on issues that are not a priority to your boss, for example.

- Bring solutions, not problems, to your boss, and look for opportunities to make his or her job easier.

- Understand the organization's overall strategy and prioritize your own work accordingly. Take advantage of (and engineer) conversations with senior managers to clarify objectives and to communicate successes. Timed correctly, an opportune meeting at the coffee machine can provide a good way to raise your profile and bolster your perceived value.

- If you suspect that your stock within the organization is slipping, do something about it. Look for new opportunities internally – or make a decision to move on.

LIFESTYLE DECISIONS: 'DOWNSHIFTING'

Imported from the US, 'downshifting' is a term applied to managers and other professional people who decide to shift down a gear in their working lives, in order to enjoy a more relaxed lifestyle. Anyone considering following John Ruscoe's example, however, should think long and hard before taking the plunge.

In 1987, tired of commuting every day from his home near Stoke to his company's office in Manchester, John Ruscoe turned his back on the rat race. He and his wife left their home in North Staffordshire for an 80 hectare (200-acre) farm on Orkney. Today, he combines his job as a software engineer with sheepfarming.

Ruscoe is one of a growing number of teleworkers who have managed to make their jobs fit with their chosen lifestyle in the Highlands and Islands of Scotland. His story, which featured in a TV commercial for his employer ICL, offers a ray of hope for jaded commuters everywhere.

'When the software design office where I worked was moved to Manchester, I had an hour and a half journey in each direction', he explains. 'I got fed up with that. I felt there was something better I could do with those three hours every day.'

According to the government development agency Highlands and Islands Enterprise (HIE), too, Ruscoe's story isn't as unusual as you might think. Says Jon Poore, HIE's press officer:

> 'There are now about 700 teleworkers in the Highlands and Islands. Among them are software designers and translators, as well as a wide range of companies. That makes us the UK hub for remote working.'

As companies step up their search to escape the high cost of city centre offices in the coming years, too, HIE believes the region offers the ideal 21st century business location.

Elsewhere, teleworkers in the Western Isles are helping the Metropolitan Police fight crime by compiling a forensic database, while others employed by the Highland-based company Crossaig provide a medical database for Dutch publishing giant Elsevier. A number of telecottages also provide business and training services to local firms in the region.

Yet the technology to do teleworking has been around for many years. ICL, for example, first used the technique back in 1970. As John Ruscoe explains:

> *'People think it can only work if you work in IT, but really the technology doesn't have to be that sophisticated. All you need is a telephone, a PC and a modem. I think the attitude of the company is actually the most important thing.*

Does he miss the office?

> *'Not really, although I do sometimes think I miss out on the little things. What I call "office osmosis." The interesting little conversations you overhear. The person sitting next to the one you're talking to on the telephone, for instance, could be working on something really interesting without you ever knowing.*
>
> *'It's not all fairy-tale stuff. It rains most of the time, it's cold even in the summer and there's very little daylight in the winter. Anyone who has seen 'The Good Life' on television and thinks it's easy is likely to be disappointed. If the tractor's conked out, you know you're the only person who's going to fix it. You just have to get on with it.*
>
> *'Our decision to move was two or three years in the planning. All that time I was reading books about farming and making sure everything was as failsafe as possible so that if everything went badly wrong I could go back to Manchester. You don't make a lot of money from a farm this size. That was why it was essential to get myself organized like this. Working this way I can have the lifestyle I want.'*

HEALTH DECISIONS

We can't all pack up and head off to the Highlands and Islands of Scotland, of course. But we can all make the decision to put our health and well-being first. That means deciding on a balanced lifestyle.

A balanced lifestyle takes account of a number of factors to find a formula which we are comfortable with:

- family
- job
- career (not necessarily the same thing as current job)
- health
- hobbies and other interests.

The pressure at work these days means that many of us work too many hours, don't get enough exercise and neglect the other areas of our lives. In recent years, however, there have been moves to redress this imbalance by educating managers through so-called 'wellness programmes'. Some business schools even offer programmes for senior managers to help them achieve a balanced lifestyle.

Ashridge School of Management in Berkhamsted, Hertfordshire, for example, runs a programme called 'Lifestyle planning for performance'. It is the brainchild of John Neal, fitness coach to the Middlesex Cricket Club (MCC) and consultant to a string of business organizations.

> 'This isn't a fitness course. Lifestyle planning is a method of avoiding burn-out. It's a balancing act; a way of balancing what you need to do with what you'd like to do. I do a lot of work with cardiac rehabs. They're very receptive to these ideas because they've had a scare. The point of this programme is to say don't wait until you've had a heart attack at 45 or 50, plan now to avoid it.'

Lifestyle planning, however, involves more than just joining a health club. It is a decision about the way you want to live your life. It should combine career choices, with health and happiness.

According to Ina Smith, a consultant psychologist at Ashridge Consulting Ltd, the consulting arm of Ashridge School of Management, lifestyle planning should involve both the physiological and psychological aspects – the body and the mind.

> 'It should be a holistic approach. It's about standing back and assessing how well your lifestyle meets your needs.
>
> 'Most executives don't have much time for themselves. The typical lifestyle involves long hours, high workloads, poor eating habits – either grabbing something to eat in a taxi or a lavish business lunch – and often insomnia. People adopt a negative attitude to the pressures – drinking too much, for example, or eating too much. But there are more positive approaches. By paying more attention to their coping strategies they can increase their feeling of well-being, feel more in control and at the same time improve their work performance . It's for people who want to live beyond 60.'

Increasing concern about the workloads of UK managers make the advice especially timely. Some 71 million days are currently lost in Britain each year through stress-related illness, with an average cost of £12,000 per company.

References

1. Reilly, P, and Tamkin, P, *Outsourcing: A flexible option for the future?*, Institute for Emploment Studies, 1996.

2. Lacity, M, and Willcocks, L, *Best Practice in Information Technology Sourcing*, Oxford Executive Research Briefings, Templeton College, Oxford University, 1996.

Afterword

As explained in the introduction, the aim of this book has been to help managers develop better decision-making habits. In the end, though, it is the skill and judgement of managers that will determine the success of decisions. My final piece of advice is, to borrow the words of an unknown sage:

'If it be right, do it boldly, if it be wrong leave it undone.'

Bibliography

Barker, Alan, *How to be a Better Decision-maker*, Kogan Page, 1996.

Belasco, James A, *Teaching the Elephant to Dance*, Century, 1990.

Brake, Terence, *The Global Leader*, Irwin, 1997.

Chonko, Lawrence B, *Ethical Decision-making in Marketing*, Sage, 1995.

Clutterbuck, David, and Goldsmith, Walter, *The Winning Streak Mark II*, Orion, 1997.

Clutterbuck, David, and Dearlove, Des, 'The Charity as a Business', *Directory of Social Change*, 1996.

Crainer, Stuart, *Key Management Ideas*, Pitman, 1996.

Crainer, Stuart, *The Ultimate Business Library*, Capstone, 1997.

Dawson, Roger, *Make the Right Decision Every Time*, Nicholas Brealey, 1994.

de Bono, E, *Future Positive*, Penguin, 1983.

Deep, Sam, and Sussman, Lyle, *Smart Moves for People in Charge*, Addison-Wesley, 1995.

de Vries, M Kets, and Dick, R, *Branson's Virgin: The coming of age of a counter-cultural enterprise*, INSEAD, Fontainebleau, 1995.

Drucker, Peter, *Management: Tasks, Responsibilities, Practices*, Harper and Row, New York, 1974.

Drummond, Helga, *Effective Decision-making*, (2nd edition) Kogan Page, 1996.

Geus, Arie, de, *The Living Company*, Nicholas Brealey, 1997.

Glass, Neil, *Management Masterclass*, Nicholas Brealey, 1996.

Hammer, M, and Champy, J, *Re-engineering the Corporation*, Harper Business, New York, 1993.

Handy, C, *The Future of Work*, Basil Blackwell, Oxford, 1984.

Handy, C, *The Age of Unreason*, Century Business Books, London, 1989.

Kanter, R M, '*When Giants Learn to Dance*', Simon and Schuster, 1989.

Kleiner, Art, *The Age of Heretics*, Nicholas Brealey, 1996.

Koch, Richard, and Godden, Ian, *Managing Without Management*, Nicholas Brealey, 1996.

Koch, Richard, *The 80/20 Principle*, Nicholas Brealey, 1997.

Kouzes, James M, and Posner, Barry S, *Credibility: How leaders gain and lose it; why people demand it*, Jossey-Bass, San Francisco, 1993.

Lacity, Mary, and Willcocks, Leslie, *Best Practice in Information Technology Sourcing*, Oxford Executive Research Briefings, Templeton College, Oxford University, 1996.

Nonaka, I, and Takeuchi, H, *The Knowledge-creating Company: How Japanese companies create the dynamics of innovation*, Oxford University Press, 1995.

Parikh, Jagdish, *Intuition: The new frontier of management*, Blackwell, Oxford, 1994.

Pascale, Richard, *Managing on the Edge*, Simon and Schuster, New York, 1990.

Peters, Tom, *Thriving on Chaos*, Macmillan, London, 1987.

Peters, Tom, *Liberation Management*, Knopf, 1992.

Porter, Michael, *Competitive Strategy: Techniques for analyzing industries and competitors*, Free Press, New York, 1980.

Schein, E H, *Organizational Culture and Leadership*, Jossey-Bass, San Francisco, 1985.

Senge, P, *The Fifth Discipline: The art and practice of the learning organization*, Doubleday, New York, 1990.

Senge, P, with Roberts, C, Ross, R, Smith, B, and Kleiner, A, *The Fifth Discipline Field Book: Strategies and tools for building a learning organization'*, Nicholas Brealey, 1994.

Sloan, A P, *My Years with General Motors*, Doubleday, New York, 1963.

Smith, Hyrum W, *The 10 Laws of Successful Time and Life Management*, Nicholas Brealey, 1994.

Stewart, Thomas A, *Intellectual Capital: The new wealth of organizations*, Nicholas Brealey, 1997.

Taylor, F W, *The Principles of Scientific Management*, Harper and Row, New York, 1911.

Trompenaars, Fons, *Riding the Waves of Culture*, Nicholas Brealey, 1993.

Van Gunsteren, L, *FT Handbook of Management,* Pitman, 1995.

Wagner, R, and Sternberg, R, 'Street Smarts', in *Measures of Leadership*, Clark, K, and Clark, M, (editors) Leadership Library of America, West Orange NJ, 1990.

White, R P, Hodgson, P, and Crainer, S, *The Future of Leadership*, Pitman, 1996.

Index